PUTTING LOVE TO WORK IN MARRIAGE

♥♥♥♥♥♥♥♥♥♥♥♥

God bless you,
Terri Robinson Williams

PUTTING LOVE TO WORK IN MARRIAGE

♥♥♥♥♥♥♥♥♥♥♥♥

Charles P. De Santo
and
Terri Robinson Williams

HERALD PRESS
Scottdale, Pennsylvania
Kitchener, Ontario

Library of Congress Cataloging-in-Publication Data

De Santo, Charles.
    Putting love to work in marriage / Charles P. De Santo and Terri Robinson Williams.
    p. cm.
    Bibliography: p.
    Includes indexes.
    ISBN 0-8361-3471-0 (pbk.)
    1. Marriage—United States. 2. Marriage—Religious aspects—Christianity. 3. Love. I. Williams, Terri Robinson, 1958- II. Title.
HQ734.D39 1988
646.7'8—dc19   88-11194
                                                                               CIP

Except as otherwise indicated, Scripture is taken from the *Holy Bible: New International Version*, copyright © 1973, 1978, 1984 by the International Bible Society. Used by permission of Zondervan Bible Publishers. Verses marked Phillips are from *The New Testament in Modern English*, Revised Edition, © J. B. Phillips 1958, 1960, 1972. By permission of Macmillan Publishing Co., Inc., and William Collins Sons & Co., Ltd.

PUTTING LOVE TO WORK IN MARRIAGE
Copyright © 1988 by Herald Press, Scottdale, Pa. 15683
    Published simultaneously in Canada by Herald Press,
    Kitchener, Ont. N2G 4M5. All rights reserved.
Library of Congress Catalog Card Number: 88-11194
International Standard Book Number: 0-8361-3471-0
Printed in the United States of America
Design by Jim Butti

94 93 92 91 90 89 88 10 9 8 7 6 5 4 3 2 1

*To Beth and Troy Turner
who demonstrated
that the love and grace of God
was more than sufficient
for their every need.*

CONTENTS

Authors' Preface 9
Acknowledgments 12

1. Suffering in Marriage: Minimizing the Stress 15
2. Religion in Marriage: Believing the "Right Stuff" 30
3. Expectations in Marriage: Adjusting to Reality 44
4. Love in Marriage: A Way of Behaving 60
5. Communication in Marriage: The Key to Growth and Happiness . . 81
6. Conflict and Anger in Marriage: Resolution and Management 96
7. Sex in Marriage: An Act of Love 104
8. Child Rearing in Marriage: Principles and Practices 118
9. Infidelity in Marriage: Push and Pull Factors 137

Notes 155
Study and Discussion Questions 157
Suggested Readings 173
Bibliography 177
Scripture Index 179
General Index 181
The Authors 187

AUTHORS' PREFACE

All marriages can be improved. If we are happily married, we want to do all that we can to strengthen our relationship. If we are aware of problem areas that need attention, we want sound guidance and counsel to help resolve difficulties and differences, and to help put our marriage on a more solid foundation. If we are looking forward to marriage, then we want to know about the problem areas we will face. We also want information about principles and practices that we can discuss to help us get off to a good start in marriage.

Putting Love to Work in Marriage was written both for Christians and for those who are open to the insights that the Christian faith provides. We are both specialists in the field of family studies. We have not only taught and researched in the area of the family, but we have also counseled persons with marital and family problems. We believe that we have broken new ground in our book. While other authors have dealt with the topics we have written about, our treatment is significantly different in content, and the reader should find it most helpful. It will serve as an excellent basis for discussion between husband and wife, and for couples who are contemplating marriage. It will also provide a good background for group discussion. Questions on the content of each chapter are provided at the back of the book.

Briefly, we hold that *faith* and *love* are not merely abstract concepts or ideas, but practical, profitable ways of believing and behaving. There is no need to "suffer" as many do in marriage—even in so called good ones. If each spouse deals with problems and concerns of the present, and if both take control of their actions and live responsibly, marriage partners can improve both their individual lives and their marital relationships.

We affirm that what a person believes—one's religion—is crucial to marital harmony and happiness. Persons behave and act out what they actually believe! We maintain that what one believes about *the nature of persons* is as important as what one believes about the nature of God. Indeed, the two are inextricably related. Furthermore, we believe that *mutual servanthood* was the ideal that Christ advocated for both husband and wife. The patriarchal tradition of the New Testament ought not take precedence over teachings on mutual servanthood also clearly taught in the New Testament.

We also observe that prior expectations affect relationships within marriage. If each partner realistically trims personal expectations, adjusting to the reality of the demands of married life, this will not only reduce discord and disappointment, but also make for mutual respect and personal growth.

Love, we believe, is not merely an emotion, but *a way of behaving.* If love is to grow, it must be fed with caring, responsible behavior—much as we nurture a delicate flower. A loving attitude and a feeling of intimacy are the fruit of responsible, supportive, caring behavior.

While other books stress the importance of good communication as the key to a happy marriage, we go beyond that. *We believe that the key to good couple communication is each partner's open communication with God!* Honest communication with God makes caring communication with our spouse much easier. Realistically, we agree that all "normal people" experience conflict and get angry. We believe, however, that conflicts can be resolved, and that anger can be managed.

Sex is not only for procreation or physiological release, but is primarily a means of communicating love for one another. And it's an important, integral part of the marriage relationship. This manifestation of love, however, is often fraught with problems. We offer some suggestions for working at these. We also deal practically with the adjustments and difficulties that arise when children come into the home, reviewing some "tried and true" Christian principles of loving discipline and nurture.

Finally, we deal with the ever present temptation to be unfaithful to our wife or husband. Adultery is not something that "just happens." It is usually the end result of failure to establish a sense of *oneness* through mutually arrived at and shared goals, as well as failure to communicate well. We identify the *push* and *pull* factors that relate to fidelity and infi-

Authors' Preface

delity, and we suggest ways to help a husband and wife remain faithful.

All in all, we believe that the Christian faith embodies those principles and practices that will enable us to enrich not only our marriages, but also our personal lives.

    Charles P. De Santo   Terri Robinson Williams
    Lock Haven University   Geneva College
    Lock Haven, Pennsylvania Beaver Falls, Pennsylvania

ACKNOWLEDGMENTS

There are many to whom we are indebted as this book goes to press. Special thanks goes to Paul M. Schrock, General Book Editor at Herald Press, for his support, constructive criticisms, and encouragement. We are also grateful to Norma A. De Santo for her careful reading of the manuscript at various stages of development and for suggesting stylistic changes to make the book more readable. Janet Mann and Paul McNeely read the entire book, and Gerald Cierpilowski, David Anderson, Hugh Williamson, and Amy Carroll read several chapters. To these colleagues at the university we express our heartfelt thanks.

We are also indebted to J. Andrew Stoner (Minister of Personal and Family Life, First Mennonite Church, Berne, Ind.), William J. Peters (Director of the Family Life Bureau, Diocese of Altoona—Johnstown, Pa.) Peggy Muller (Marriage and Family Counselor-Therapist, Southeastern Counseling Center, Chattanooga, Tenn.), and John S. Muller (Professor of Sociology, Covenant College), and Robert Herron (Marriage and Family Counselor and Director of the Presbyterian Counseling Center, Greensboro, N.C.), all of whom are actively involved in marriage and family counseling, for taking time out of their busy schedules to read the book, to make some suggested changes, and to write endorsements.

Our thanks to Linda Burggraf, Donna Barton, and Peggy Fanning for typing earlier drafts of the manuscript, and to George and Gloria Zakem for preparing the final draft.

Finally, we express appreciation to our spouses whose unconditional commitment and love—which includes justice, conflict, anger, confrontation, patience, understanding, and support—enables us to work through the suffering to achieve the meaningful, positive relationship we enjoy in our marriages today.

PUTTING LOVE TO WORK IN MARRIAGE
♥♥♥♥♥♥♥♥♥♥♥

CHAPTER 1

SUFFERING IN MARRIAGE
Minimizing the Stress

Recently I spoke at a church on the topic, "You Don't Have to Suffer in Marriage." In essence, I said that all of us, whether married or single, have to learn to take suffering in stride. By suffering I mean the difficulties, personal losses, misunderstandings, illnesses, and conflicts that are inevitably a part of life. Accepting the reality of suffering and taking it in stride is the only way we can get on with the business of living and successfully cope in marriage.[1]

After the service, a woman said, "You've read *The Road Less Traveled*, haven't you?"

"No," I replied. "Should I?"

She answered, "Well, our couples group here at the church is studying it, and some of the ideas you've shared with us are similar to his."

After reading the book, it was gratifying to know that Dr. Peck expressed similar thoughts from his unique perspective as a Christian psychiatrist.[2]

Although it may be a bit startling to read at the beginning of a book entitled *Putting Love to Work in Marriage* that marriage and family life involve suffering, we encourage you to read on. For we firmly believe (and have experienced) that when we put mature love to work in our relationships suffering diminishes.

There are a variety of reasons why problems and difficulties inevitably develop in our lives. Some of the difficulties stem from the traits and behaviors that each of us brings into our marriage. Other problems emerge in the normal course of everyday life, as husbands and wives continue to grow and change—each in our unique way. Still others develop as we work at trying to mesh and integrate these changes. Often we don't understand these new traits and behaviors. But we soon learn that there's no magic way to bring about marital harmony other than by hard work on the part of both partners—by compromising and accommodating differences.

We also learn that successful marriage includes giving our spouse his or her own space. Husbands and wives need the freedom to develop their own unique personal gifts and abilities. And we need to accept each other's quirks—the traits we like, as well as those that require adjusting to. For the unique traits each of us possesses are the very things that make us the special people we are.

While we believe that suffering *is* a part of our human condition, we also believe that much of it can be reduced and prevented *if* we keep our marital goals clearly before us, and *if* we're willing to put mature love to work.

A Basic Concept

There is no aspect of marital relations to which Christian love or caring are not applicable or relevant. We are not talking about the popular concept of romantic love that permeates Western society, and is portrayed profusely by the mass media. Romantic love is grossly sensual and erotic in nature. It portrays men and women "thinking with their genitals." It is highly self-centered and motivated largely by an intense desire for excitement and erotic sexual satisfaction. While we believe that sexual intimacy is a natural, desirable, and integral part of most good marriages, it certainly is not the whole of a loving relationship. Romantic love as portrayed in novels, movies, and on TV gives us an unrealistic notion of what marital relationships are all about.

Furthermore, we cannot sustain a "romantic high." Romantic love includes a good bit of fantasy. It's often self-centered, rather than other-centered. It asks, "What kind of excitement and pleasure will I receive from this relationship?"

When we speak of love or caring, we have in mind the ideal concept of Christian love *(agape)*, the altruistic love that is best demonstrated in the redemptive action of God when he sent Christ to redeem us. As we experience God's unmerited grace, God calls us to act out this unselfish kind of love in our relationships with others. And this acting out of love for others begins right in our homes, in our marital and family relationships (1 Timothy 5:8).

Agape love is the kind of love that Troy and Beth shared beautifully for six years. Troy met Beth while he was in college. They courted for three years before they married. Beth worked outside the home while Troy finished his B.A. in philosophy, graduating with honors. They moved to Boston, where Troy began studying for his M.Div. degree. During his first year there, Troy was stricken with cancer of the sinus cavity. For the next two years he was in and out of the hospital and seminary. He waged a valiant fight against the disease. Through it all, his beloved and faithful wife stood by him. In addition to the common problems and difficulties all married couples share, they also bore the burden brought on by the physical suffering of the cancer.

Through the operation and hospital stays, their commitment to God and to each other grew. A little more than a year before Troy died, he spoke at church, saying, "I know that my illness did not take God by surprise!" He went on to say that God had a plan for his life. He knew that God could heal him, if he wished to. But whether God did or not, he was committed to serving God.

After a year had passed Troy spoke in church again. His health had deteriorated. This time he had to sit as he spoke. He said, "I know that the sufferings of this present time are not worth comparing with the glory that is to be revealed in us." Troy did not think that because he was a Christian, he would be exempted from physical pain and suffering. He accepted life's problems, difficulties, and his illness as part of the human experience. While he didn't regard *all* things as good, he and Beth firmly believed "that in all things God works for the good of those who love him, who have been called according to his purpose" (Romans 8:28). Beth and Troy accepted life as it came to them. And they were more than conquerors because of the agape love they shared with God and with one another!

Christian love is superior to the modern pop psychology that counsels us to "look out for number one." Such advice is merely a license for narcissism, for excessive and unhealthy self-love. It does not permit us to achieve the *oneness* Christ set forth as the ideal—a oneness many of us have experienced and in which we strive to grow (Mark 10:7-9). Putting oneself before *all* others is nothing less than idolatry. At least "primitives" who worshiped idols did not deify themselves. In that sense their religion was a healthier paganism than that of many contemporary Americans. From a Christian perspective, we cannot be spiritually and psychologically healthy if our goal in life is to "look out for number one." We are *social* beings who only find meaning, satisfaction, and happiness when we are rightly related to God and others.

Our Christian Beliefs

As mature people, we realize that we cannot make another person happy. Others are responsible for their own happiness. We choose when and how we will be happy. In the Christian faith, happiness comes to us as we act right—when we live by the principles of Christ. One of the basic teachings of our faith is that we are responsible for our own actions and feelings (Ezekiel 18:1-4).

Cathy was a faithful wife and mother, who had no time for hobbies, nor did she work outside of the home. Her husband, however, was busy with his work, as well as with sports and other interests. Cathy felt lonely and depressed. At first she blamed her husband, but her counselor helped her to see that she had to take charge of her own life. She began doing ceramics with other women and became active in the work of the local church. Not only did her depression leave, but her husband also found her to be a more stimulating person to be with.

While we cannot make someone else happy, it's important to realize that we are obligated to live responsibly, and thereby facilitate the growth of our spouse.

It may sound paradoxical, but it's true. We are our brother's and sister's helper. Christ commanded us to love our neighbor as ourselves, and to do for others what we would like them to do for us. In marriage, this means that we will do those things that free up time so that our spouse can do some of the things that are meaningful to him or her.

Larry had dumped all the nurturing responsibility on his wife, so that Grace had no time to herself. She loved playing in the community orchestra, but she had given it up. After a few sessions of counseling, their pastor helped Larry to see the unfairness of the family situation. Larry began to assume more responsibility around the house. His wife not only had time to practice her flute, but also to return to the community orchestra. When Larry lived more responsibly, both he and Grace benefited.

Living responsibly also means that we will not take over those tasks that our spouse should rightfully assume. This would not only deprive the spouse of independence, self-respect, and responsibility, but it would also interfere with personal development. Neither the husband who dominates his wife, making all decisions unilaterally, nor the wife who waits on her husband hand and foot is building a good marriage relationship. Love and mutual respect are best shown by striking that delicate balance between being overly solicitous and being unconcerned.

We experience love through our relationship to God in Christ. Then, through the power and grace of God's Spirit, we work at sharing this love with others. Relationships are the key—relationships with God and others. We profit most when both relationships are sustained and nourished simultaneously. If they are not, we become unbalanced. Failing to maintain a balance results in hypocrisy and a religious experience lacking in vitality and joy. It can also lead to strain and stagnation in marriage. Only when we maintain both the vertical relationship with God and the horizontal relationship with others, can we begin to fulfill the great commandment (Mark 12:29-31).

Difficulties, Struggles, and Suffering

But we all know that even when we love God and sincerely try to put love to work in marriage, we still struggle and have difficulties and conflicts that result in stress. Why?

One reason is that even though as Christians we have found forgiveness and new life in Christ, as humans we still fall into sin and offend both God and others. Even at our best we are still sinful, finite creatures. When Christ died and rose from the dead, he was taken up into heaven. But when we die with Christ and rise with him to newness of life, we must still live our lives here on earth. We still have to struggle with the weakness of the flesh and temptations. We still have to struggle with our human condition. Conflicts and problems remain an inherent part of our experience.

Another reason we experience difficulties is that we often confuse basic Christian teaching. Many tend to think that since God's grace is free, the fruit of the Spirit can be obtained without effort. While we believe that salvation is the free gift of God, we can never forget that its cost was tremendous—the death of God's Son. Likewise, while the fruit of the Spirit is offered to us freely, acquiring the attributes of love, joy, peace, patience, kindness, goodness, faithfulness, gentleness, and self-control (Galatians 5:22) demands hard, persistent work on the part of each of us. It doesn't come without effort. That is why Jesus commanded us to love (John 13:34; 15:12). The fulfillment of the "royal law" of the kingdom is not easy. But the fruit is worth the intense effort required. Not only will our relationship with the living God deepen, but these spiritual fruits will also enrich our marriage.

Jesus never said that happiness and fulfillment in life would come without effort (Matthew 7:14). In fact, he plainly stated that there is a "yoke" to bear (Matthew 11:29). But since the rewards of obedience to his teachings are so great, the effort we put forth doesn't seem burdensome. As we grow and develop in our spiritual lives and as the fruit of the Spirit becomes evident in us, the burden diminishes. Nevertheless, the yoke and the responsibility still remain. The apostle Paul advised us to work out our salvation with fear and trembling (Philippians 2:12-13). This includes working out loving relationships within the family.

Another reason we have difficulty in marriage is that we allow our pride to lead us to rebel against the known will of God. Unfortunately, just as Adam and Eve rebelled against God, allowing pride to challenge God's commands, so we are often deceived and blinded by pride. We find it difficult to bend our wills to God's. Such pride and rebellion result in our estrangement from God and our nearest neighbor—our husband or wife. It is difficult to put love to work when we are in a state of rebellion against God.

Pride was Tom's problem. He had left his wife, Kathy, and their two children. After a couple years of "living it up," things began to turn sour. A friend invited him to church where he was confronted and challenged by the claims of Christ. Tom was ready to face God and himself. He decided it was time to stop running from God—time to set aside his pride, to repent of his sins, and begin to live responsibly. His decision resulted not only in reconciliation to God through faith in Christ, but also in Tom and Kathy and the two children being reunited. Today Tom knows the joy that comes from humility before God.

We are not suggesting for a moment that as Christians neither Tom nor we have a problem with pride. But once we acknowledge that it is a problem, we can deal with it.

In summary, much of the suffering we experience in marriage is due to our human condition, our failure to put love to work, and our failure to deal realistically with the profound grip that pride exerts on us. The anguish we experience stems from one or more of the above three reasons. But there is a cure. The cure is found in the Word of God and in God's power, the power of his Holy Spirit at work within us.

Being Aware of Our Beliefs

A realistic approach to marriage renewal and growth calls for ridding ourselves of certain false ideas and accepting "the facts of life."

First, it's helpful to get rid of the idea that there are couples who do not have conflict and stress in their marriages. There are no couples who live in "perfect wedded bliss." Mature people realize that while marriages may be "made in heaven," they must be worked out on earth. This means struggling with the inevitable problems that arise because of our finitude and human weakness.

Occasionally we meet those who say, "We have a perfect marriage! We never fight." Perhaps. But likely when people talk like that, one spouse is completely subservient (living in a master/slave relationship), or is rooster- or hen-pecked! The good marriage is not one that is free of conflicts, but one in which husbands and wives resolve differences to their mutual satisfaction.

Unfortunately, though there is no evidence to support the myth of a "perfect marriage," the myth persists. One reason is because somehow we think that Christians ought to be perfect and, therefore, Christian marriages should be perfect too (Matthew 5:48). Jesus, however, never suggested that we could become sinless. When the context of Jesus' statement is examined we see that he was commanding us to "be good" to *all* people.

Another reason the myth persists is that we usually see couples when they are "on stage," at their best. We seldom see them when they are anxious, tired, arguing, and torn between conflicting values and goals, and competing claims for their time and resources. It's probably a good thing we don't. If we did, we'd likely be shocked. What we would find if we looked "back stage" is that the ideal couple who appears ever so sweet and charming in public, wrestle with the same sort of problems we do. They have difficulty communicating. They argue about sexual matters,

Minimizing the Stress 23

money, in-laws, and children. They have their ups and downs, their highs and lows.

Alice complains George never listens, takes her for granted.

Fred complains about Brenda's constant nagging.

Brian has a hot temper, but his wife, Eve, pouts until he gives in to her wishes.

When Tony and Jean become angry, they give each other the "silent treatment."

Obviously, all marriage partners don't have the same problems. But we can be sure, if both husband and wife are alive and growing, that problems, differences, and misunderstandings which create stress are a part of their experience. Some couples, unfortunately, allow their problems to overwhelm them. But many sincerely try to work through their difficulties and continue the adventure and growth process.

Second, once we accept the fact that growth means change, and that change is often a bit painful, we can handle it and grow both as a couple and personally. Change is especially painful when we are the ones who have to do the changing, when we are the ones giving up some behavior that our spouse may find destructive or offensive.

We are not suggesting for a moment that we must lose our identities. But if we are to achieve the kind of oneness we desire, someone has to give. As the family changes, as we go through the various stages in the family life cycle, changes must take place if we are to meet one another's needs.

We often find it difficult coping with changes in our spouse, even good changes. We become accustomed to the behaviors and characteristics of our spouse, and we may find changes unsettling. Even when these changes are positive, we may experience feelings of insecurity because our wife or husband is not who he or she once was. We get used to our spouse's established behaviors and responses—we depend on things remaining the same. But when we love persons as Christ loves them, the positive growth that leads to change must be our wish for them.

Third, even under the best of circumstances, marriage and family life involve suffering. This may not be the result of a specific "sin," but may simply emerge from the problems and difficulties that we encounter as humans. We're not omniscient—we don't know everything. God alone knows all! As wives or husbands it's helpful to be understanding and supportive when our spouse makes a mistake in judgment. On those occasions when we misunderstand one another, and hurt one another, it's not a sign that love is absent. For try as we may, these things will happen.

We are not suggesting that we take a casual attitude toward one another's shortcomings and offenses. By no means. But some of the pain is diffused when we realize that in the inevitable give-and-take within marriage and family life, some suffering will be experienced. To some extent, the suffering experienced is a sign that growth is taking place and both are playing an equally vital role in the relationship. Naturally, as we learn more about how to adapt to each other and to please one another, the amount of suffering will diminish.

Fourth, even in good marriages, it's good to take time out for periodic checkups. It's essential to stop and ask, "What have I been doing that is right, or wrong?" And, "What have we failed to do that needs to be done?" We need to think through where we hope to go in our marriage—to set goals.

Martha was a strong-willed, dominant person when she married Mike. She tried to control most aspects of their life together. Being in control gave her a sense of security, but her criticisms and demands began to deflate Mike's optimistic and upbeat personality. Mike became withdrawn and depressed. Through Scripture reading and interaction with friends, as well as her pastor, Martha became aware of what she was doing. She realized that she had to change if she did not want to lose her husband, and if growth was to take place in their marriage. Change wasn't easy because she had to give up old ways. But with strength gained through prayer, Martha was able to change and their marriage began to improve.

If people in business and industry, as well as churches, utilize evaluative tools to measure the productivity and effectiveness of workers and executives, how much more should we in the family? Joseph and Lois Bird repeatedly make the point that husbands and wives need to get away by themselves to renew their marriage.[3] We owe it to each other to step back occasionally and take stock together of the areas in our marriage that need strengthening. Such times also give us the opportunity to celebrate our strengths—to thank God and each other for the gift of one another.

We have never met a couple whose marriage has not been strengthened by getting away by themselves. If the idea is new to you, start with a marriage encounter or enrichment weekend, and then move on to your own program.

Eliminate the Negative

In addition to getting rid of mistaken ideas about marriage, there are some definite affirmations we can make. We can begin to take charge of our marriage by taking the following steps. These will help eliminate negative practices that stand in the way of achieving oneness and happiness.

First, we can affirm our husband or wife as the one whom God, in his providence, has led us to choose as a mate. Since we believe this, there is no justification for making uncomplimentary comparisons between our marriage and that of others. Making such comparisons are not only a put-down of our spouse, but they obstruct progress in our own marriage. We are not denying that we often are helped by observing those who model behaviors we may wish to copy, but this is something quite different from using others to put down our spouse. If we want to improve our own marriage, it's best to concentrate on what *is*, and how we can go about accomplishing the desired change.

Jim learned this lesson the hard way. He was constantly pointing to "other wives" and what they did and how they dressed and behaved. Joy had finally had enough. She decided that two could play the game. When she began comparing Jim to "other husbands," he got the message and apologized. They both decided to turn their energies to being supportive and encouraging of each other.

Making comparisons is of questionable usefulness. What works and looks good in other marriages may not work for us. Each marriage is a unique relationship between two of God's "one-of-a-kind" people. The strengths in our marriage may be quite different from those of other marriages.

Second, we can accept responsibility for our own behavior and realize that we bear the primary responsibility for improving our marital relationship. It's unprofitable to blame others for our present troubles. Blaming others helps no one, least of all our spouse! Establishing blame—saying, "it's one's parents', spouse's, child's, or the boss's fault"—does not change the present situation one iota. Blaming only lays guilt on others and compounds our problems. Furthermore, it keeps us from squarely facing our own shortcomings and from working to eliminate them. Realistically, I am the only person I can change, and *you* are the only person *you* can change. Jesus said the way to improve a relationship is to improve our own vision. We do this by removing the log from our own eye, not by taking the splinter from our spouse's eye.

Of course we do suffer from the irresponsible actions or failure of others. And surely we also have caused others to suffer. But what is past *is* past! The helpful thing to do is to accept the challenge and opportunities of our present situation.

Third, there is nothing to be gained by saying to ourselves, "If only I had done *this* instead of *that!* If only I had chosen *that* instead of *this!* If only I had gone *there* instead of *here!*" While reflecting upon the past can be helpful, obsession with what might have been is an utter waste of valuable time and energy.

Mature, sensible people concern themselves with the present. Forget the past! Oneness in marriage can never be achieved unless we close the door on what might have been.

If we are going to be productive in life, as well as in marriage, we need to work at it now with what gifts and abilities God has given us. As John Gile put it in his *Minute Meditation:*

> The illusion
>   that there will be some time in the future
>   when all things will come together for us
>   interferes with our fully living today.
> If we aren't living fully now,
>   we never will.
> The only time we have is the present.

Fourth, in affirming our husband or wife, we should not waste time speculating on how things might have been if we had married someone else. Of what value is this? Things would probably not be significantly better if we had married someone else. Why? Because *I* would still take *me,* and *you* would still take *you* into that other marriage. If we took the *same self* into the marriage that might have been, is there really any reason to believe that the marriage would be significantly different? That other person whom we speculate about would also bring with him or her weaknesses and quirks that would require the same type of adjustment and work that your present relationship demands. The sensible thing to do, therefore, is to get on with the important business of changing the present marriage.

Finally, marriage enrichment requires that we primarily dwell on the positive and possible, and that we set aside all negative ideas that might hinder growth. Such ideas may include fear of failure, dwelling on the minor faults of the spouse, or thinking that change is impossible. Enrichment requires renewing the faith and love that brought the two of us together. After all, we are intelligent people. We would not have married the spouse we did unless we believed that he or she was a "good catch." Maybe it was her smile, her figure, her superior intellect, and her strength of character that appealed to you. Or maybe it was his patience, his sensitivity, his understanding nature, his sense of humor, his physique or his aspirations that impressed you. The fact is that at that time you believed you were meant for each other.

How Marriages Change

If our marriage is not what we think it ought to be at this time, it is probably because our attitudes and behaviors have changed. During courtship we worked hard to win each other's affection. We did it by doing the things that pleased one another. But once married, we allow the cares of everyday life to absorb most of our time. We have a tendency to take each other for granted, and not work as hard at pleasing one another. Some of the altruism and unselfishness gives way to egotism and selfishness. But despite this, the love is still there. The flame of love has not gone out, although it may only be burning dimly because of all the debris we have laid on it. But let's not dwell on the past. It's what we do from now on that counts—and that is up to you and me. If we are ready to recommit ourselves to nurturing the relationship, we can remove the debris and do those things that will cause the dimly burning flame to burn more brightly.

If we hope to renew our marriages, maximum growth results *when both* husbands and wives commit themselves to working at it. There are many analogies that we could use, but let's draw on the insights provided by the game of tennis. We can't play tennis by ourselves. The game requires two willing, enthusiastic partners. In that sense, marriage is like tennis. Love must be reciprocated or returned if the "game" is to keep going. If one partner refuses to return the ball, the game stops. When the ball is in your court, it must be returned. At times you may hit the ball swiftly and at other times you may just send an easy lob. Sometimes you play the ball close to the net, and at other times you don't. But so long as both keep at the game, while it may prove to be tiring and trying at times, it will always be stimulating and rewarding. And so it is in marriage when *both* put love to work.

So here we are, married to a man or a woman to whom God, in his providence, has led us to make a commitment. If we have closed the door on the past, on all that might otherwise have been, and if we have covenanted with God and each other to put love to work—then we can begin to take the steps needed to renew our love for one another. Let us begin by claiming the promises of God. He has given us the power of his indwelling Spirit to enable us to renew our vows and to go on to discover new joy and happiness in our marriage. The next move is ours.

CHAPTER 2

RELIGION IN MARRIAGE
Believing the "Right Stuff"

What is your "religion?" We all have one, you know. While it may come as a shock to some, it's true.[1] Our religion consists of the set of *beliefs* we hold about reality (about what we think is true or false about anything in the universe). Our beliefs, in turn, determine our *values* (ideas about what is important in life).

Because religion is so important we have placed this chapter early in the book. While it is a bit heavy, it provides the groundwork for the rest of the book. Read it carefully, because it provides the biblical background for the "more practical" chapters that follow.

Many of our beliefs cannot be proven or shown in a material way, but they are real to us. It is these beliefs that constitute our *assumptions*. Everybody has them: the *theist*—the person who believes in God; the *atheist*—the person who does not believe that God exists; and the *agnostic*—the person who does not know whether there is a God or not. Assumptions are matters of *faith*, beliefs that we assume to be true. William L. Smith-Hinds observes that there are four ways to pursue truth. Each of the four—scientific, rational, intuitive, and revealed—make a contribution to our knowledge and life.[2] Usually all four play a part in the development of our philosophy of being, our spirituality, and our sense of personhood.

Behavior Reveals Beliefs

If someone said to you, "Tell me what you believe," how would you respond? Probably most of us could explain what we believe about God, the nature of persons, and what we think is important in life—our values. And many of us are aware of the fact that our beliefs motivate us to behave the way we do.

Some may protest, "But I'm not religious! I don't have anything to do with the church!" But if we go to their friends, they could soon tell us from having observed their daily behavior and from listening to them talk, just what their religion is—even though it may not be Christianity. People can tell what our values and beliefs are simply by watching us, because our behavior reflects them.

They might say such things as: "He's prejudiced!" "She certainly is materialistic, isn't she?" "He's really a loving husband and father, isn't he?" "Isn't it nice how they seem to do a lot as a family. They're close!" "They are consistent Christians. They not only attend church but they actively help others in need." "That young fellow certainly is a trustworthy person, isn't he?" (One sure way others can tell what our beliefs and values are is by looking at our canceled checks!)

Yes, all of us have a religion, a set of beliefs, by which we live. We define religion as *that set of beliefs about reality that becomes the driving force in our life.* It doesn't necessarily have to include belief in God or a supreme being.

We believe that religion is *the primary influence* in one's life. It not only shapes our view of the world, but it also becomes the building blocks for our personal life. Once we choose our religion and take it to heart, its influence is profound and pervasive.

We realize that this has to be qualified somewhat. All of us have shortcomings that we are trying hard to shake—habits that run counter to our religious profession. These may include a physical problem like gluttony, smoking, or alcoholism that is ruining our health or a spiritual problem such as envy, jealousy, lack of self-control, pride, or ingratitude that affects both our physical and spiritual health. While we try to overcome the problem and make our actions match our religious beliefs, we seem to be powerless to change. What are we to make of this inconsistency? Do we really want to get rid of the problem? Or do we secretly enjoy it? No, we really do want to change, but...

Most of us would agree that our behavior tells others what we really believe and what we really think is important in life. After all, we are free to do as we please, aren't we?

Healthy Religion

Based on counseling and observation, as well as numerous studies, we believe that healthy religion makes a positive contribution to marriage and family life.[3] When we speak of healthy religion, we mean the Judeo-Christian faith as set forth in the historic creeds, confessions, and theologies of Christendom—Protestant and Catholic.[4]

It is not enough, however, to give *mental assent* to the notion that God exists. We must do more than simply think that God exists. A pastor once asked one of his inactive members who said that she believed in God, "What does your God expect of you?" She replied, "Nothing." Faith like that is no faith at all. It is not a helpful force in one's life. Belief or faith must be *active*. Indeed, active faith is the only authentic kind of faith. For if we merely acknowledge God intellectually, we are guilty of practical atheism.

It is important not only to believe that God exists, but that he has revealed his purposes for us in the Old and New Testaments, which serve as our guide for living. It is helpful to turn to the Bible for insight and guidance. When we do, God's Spirit enables us to apply his truths to our life. The only requirement is an open heart and mind.

Many who withdraw from involvement in the church naively believe that they have withdrawn from religion. Wrong! They still have *religious beliefs* and a way of life that includes *set rituals*. While they do not spell God with a capital "g" they still have *a* god. And this god serves as a driving force in their lives. It might be work, athletics, money, possessions, lust, the club, the business, or another person. Unfortunately, devotion to such things do not make for wholeness in our personal or family life. Voltaire was right. People are incurably religious. But we believe that only a genuine Christian faith can make a person whole. As St. Augustine said, we are restless until we find our rest in God. God alone enables us to stand on our own two feet.

At the outset, it is important to get things in proper perspective by letting God be God. The God we worship and serve exists beyond the limits of our humanness, yet he lives within us. There is always the danger that we attempt to make God in our own image—a mere human god with no power or authority, with all the limitations and frailties we have. This we must avoid. The only God worthy of our worship and service is the God revealed in Scripture—particularly in the life and teachings of Jesus Christ. This God is all powerful, and has made us in his image.

The Nature of God

God is love, and his love is seen in all of his attributes: *creator, redeemer, judge, guide,* and *sustainer.* In love God created us. In love God redeems or rescues us. God does this in a variety of ways throughout our life, as well as in that once-for-all act of redemption through the life-death-resurrection-ascension of his Son, Jesus Christ.

In addition, in love God displays his justice as he judges us. He judges us daily. His moral law prevails in the world, even though it is not always evident in the short run, or on an individual basis. It would be difficult to convince people who suffer the loss of a child or other loved ones prematurely, that we live in a world that is fair. It is difficult, also, to convince people who live under oppressive, intolerable conditions that life is fair. With numerous exceptions, however, we reap the rewards of the behavior we sow. When we do those things that we know are unjust and injurious to ourselves and others, eventually we or others pay for it. But in the short and long run, God is just. Since we believe that the grave is not the end of our existence, we have faith that someday the unknowns will be made known to us, and we will come to see that God's ways were just, fair, and loving.

The purpose of God's judgment is not to inflict pain, but to correct us and reconcile us to ourselves, others, and to himself. Just as good parents discipline their children, so God corrects us because he loves us. God disciplines us to guide us back into his righteous paths—into a fuller, more productive life.

Don saw God's judgment as a manifestation of his love. He had been captive to alcohol for over 30 years. Finally, when he reached bottom, he turned to God and found deliverance through his newly found faith in Christ and with the aid of Alcoholics Anonymous. Don didn't blame God, his wife, nor any one else for his disease. He acknowledged that he was at fault, turned his life over to God, and worked at becoming a new man. God's judgment became the means of his reconciliation to himself, his family, the community, and to God.

The Nature of Persons

The holy, transcendent, loving God created people for fellowship with himself, and with others. As children created in God's image, we have freedom of choice, the ability to create, and the ability to love and help others in their search for a satisfying life. While we are God's sons and daughters, we are still only finite people—limited in our knowledge and understanding.

As God's children, we are all equal in his sight. But we are not equally gifted. Our abilities differ. The ability to be creative and artistic, to work well with others, to organize, to be industrious, or to be humorous vary from person to person, as do wisdom and intelligence. But we can be certain of this—*all of us are ignorant about something.* We simply cannot know everything about everything or even one thing. In fact, the larger the circle of our knowledge grows, the more we become aware of the vast amount of knowledge that lies beyond the circle.

As finite humans we are also a mixture of good and evil, of

altruism and egotism. In our relationships with others we all offend in "thought, word, and deed," as the classic confessional prayer states. Understanding and accepting our finitude keeps us from pointing an accusative finger at our spouse. It frees us to work together constructively for the common good. Acknowledging our limits helps us realize the contributions our spouse and others can make to our less than perfect lives. Their input can expand our understanding of ourselves and the world around us, and help us become better persons. In humility and with gratitude we can share our strengths and weaknesses within the bonds of marriage.

Christ and Forgiveness

Through ignorance, incompetence, and willfulness, we often offend others and ourselves. In fact, the Bible teaches that when we offend self and others, we also offend God. But God in his love and mercy offers us forgiveness in Christ, and with gratitude we accept it. When we confess our sins and ask forgiveness of God and the persons we have offended, the cycle of forgiveness is completed.

But what does all this talk about God, human nature, forgiveness, and reconciliation have to do with marriage? *Everything!* Why? Because it is when we acknowledge our need, and believe that God has freely forgiven us in Christ, that we sense our obligation to forgive others—wife, husband, children, parents, in-laws, and others. In fact, we believe that forgiveness, along with love and honor, should be part of the marriage vows. Too many marriages are wrecked by partners who feel they are a cut above their spouse, self-righteous persons who feel they never make a mistake and never have to say, "I'm sorry." Invariably, those who find it difficult to apologize, also find it hard to forgive when they are offended.

The Danger of Pride

Kevin was a minister who became involved with a woman in

his parish. After a few sessions with his Christian counselor, it became clear that the counselor would not condone his infidelity and his plan to leave his wife and children. He terminated his relationship with the counselor and decided to divorce his wife. His pride blinded him to the reality of his marriage commitment and his responsibility to his family. It led him to turn a deaf ear to the voice of Scripture—which he knew all too well. He ignored the request of his wife to go with him for counseling to work out their difficulties. He also refused to answer the concerns of his adolescent children. Such is the destructive power of pride.

When we warn about pride, we are not suggesting that we should not find satisfaction in our work, in caring for our families and ourselves. We should do things to the best of our ability, being good stewards of those talents God has entrusted to us. It is healthy to have proper self-respect—valuing our life, even as God does. Through daily prayer and meditation we can ask God to make us sensitive to the needs and feelings of our spouse and others.

An Attitude of Gratitude

A grateful disposition is also an integral part of healthy religion. Christians should be positive, life affirming people—not negative, whiny, and complaining individuals. Making a habit of expressing gratitude to others and to God is physically, psychologically, and spiritually invigorating. If we were fortunate enough to have been raised in a family where parents were appreciative, then it probably comes easier for us to do so. But if we were not, we can work at cultivating this attitude.

Unfortunately, we tend to view life too much from our personal perspectives. But in marriage, as in all of life, it is not just *me* or *you*—it is *us, our, they,* and *them* also. The roots of gratitude begin when it suddenly dawns on us that "all that we are or hope to be" largely depends on the contributions others have made to us. Our personal efforts are obviously significant. But for the most part, we build on what was "given" and on what others have done. "No man (person) is an island," wrote John Donne. And the apostle Paul asks, "What do we have that we did not receive as a gift" from God and others? And if we received it as a gift, why do we boast as if it were something we accomplished on our own (1 Corinthians 4:7)? There is no room in the Christian's life for arrogance and boasting.

One way to develop the habit of expressing gratitude is by making a list of those who have contributed to our growth, noting what specific contributions they have made. Then, beginning at the top of the list, contact these persons and thank them. This is best done face-to-face. But if this is not possible, a phone call or letter will serve the purpose. It's amazing what this will do, not only for the recipient, but also for the sender.

Love and Justice

One of the central themes of the Christian religion is love. Healthy religion expresses a love modeled after God's love for us. God's love is unconditional—God gives 100%! So in marriage, our love for our spouse and children must be unconditional. This does not mean that we approve of everything they do, nor does it mean that we never get angry with one another. It does mean, that through the anger, frustration, and disappointment we never stop loving and caring. Our love for them is not based on their actions or inactions. Come what may, we will love them always.

God's love for us, although it is unconditional, includes justice. While we are grateful that God does not punish us for all of our wrongs, we thank God for the times he does correct us. God does this because he loves us. So in marriage, our love must include justice. It is *because* we love each other that we confront one another with those behaviors that work against personal and marital well-being.

Justice does not mean that we confront one another with *any* action, attitude, or behavior that strikes us as somehow difficult for us personally. Justice is getting to the heart of the behavior, weeding out the insignificant, and really working on the major problems. Negotiations that bring about change are often slow and painful. But the effort is worth it. When we recognize that justice in marital relationships is mutually beneficial, we stop trying to avoid the discomfort that may accompany communication. We set aside our pride and put love to work. Take the case of Jay and Ruth, for example.

Jay was often late for supper, largely because he was a car salesman and could not always break away by 5:00 p.m. When he came home late, his wife Ruth would light into him—berating him for being late. She would accuse him of not caring for her and the children, and of putting others before the needs of his family. The more she complained, the later he came home. Ruth's complaining was backfiring on her.

Finally, she decided to select a time when both she and Jay were relaxed to confront him with her frustration. Jay admitted that it wasn't fair for him to be late so often. But he also said that it wasn't always his fault, and besides, it wasn't pleasant coming home to a nagging wife. Ruth said that she would try to change her attitude and be more understanding and supportive. They agreed that they would have supper regularly at 6:00 p.m. for the children, and if he did not get home in time, she would feed the children and wait for him. Instead of complaining as soon as he entered the house, she asked him about his day. Gradually, Jay came home earlier and earlier. The problem was resolved when Ruth and Jay recognized the injustice each was doing to the other.

Christ's Teaching About Oneness

Another essential element of a healthy marriage is Christ's teaching that a man and a woman become one. Christ said "At the beginning of creation God 'made them male and female'" (Mark 10:6). The fullness of God is reflected not in man or woman, but in both. That is why Christ said that in marriage the two, husband and wife, are to become "one flesh" (Mark 10:8). In a real sense there are not two people, but one "new being," the married pair.

Just as the Trinity is a mystery, the unique oneness that we share in marriage is somewhat of a mystery. In good marriages the partners each retain their individuality, with each supporting the other's chosen roles and interests. It is these two hearts, minds, and lives that are growing in oneness that compose the smallest unit of the church. Christ is Lord of the church, and we look to him for guidance.

We believe that this oneness, which Christ holds up as the ideal toward which we should strive, requires 100% commitment from each partner. Commitment means that we solemnly promise to maintain and work at the marriage, as well as pledge our loyalty to our spouse. It also involves placing trust in our spouse. Christ further instructs us that this kind of commitment means that we assume a servant (supportive) role in our marriage relationship (Mark 10:44-45; John 13:1-17). In serving our spouse, both husband and wife willingly perform duties related to home and family. Each assists the other in the areas of life where one might be lacking. We work to meet the needs of our spouse—whether physical, psychological, social, or spiritual. We actively promote the interests of our spouse, supporting and encouraging a sense of fulfillment.

This is not to say that one spouse is completely subservient to the other, or that we lose the sense of self in this type of commitment and service. There is a "yours" and "mine" and an "ours" in the relationship. However, in Christian marriages, neither husband nor wife is an independent unit. We belong to each other. We try to learn all that we can about our spouse's needs and interests so that we can be the best mutual servants possible, and truly approach the divinely ordained oneness.

Of course there are some routine and mundane things that we ought to do for ourselves, such as hanging up our own clothes or cleaning out the bathtub or shower after we use it. But there are times when such things are done for the other out of love.

When Jesus calls us to a servant role, it is not to cower in fear before another, or to act as a doormat. But we are to seek to please, support, and help each other in the various roles and interests each has. As we pass through the marriage and family life cycle, we will be flexible and helpful, adapting in ways that are necessary.

Patriarchal Emphasis

We believe the church has emphasized the patriarchal tradition (the husband as head) too much. Ephesians 5:22-33 should be interpreted in the light of Ephesians 5:21. Jesus' emphasis, again, was one of *servanthood* and of being *mutually submissive* and supportive—a striving for oneness. This emphasis is also found in the apostolic teaching but we have chosen to minimize it or overlook it. Paul wrote that we are a new creation in Christ (2 Corinthians 5:17). He also taught that in Christ the barriers of race and sex come down (Galatians 3:28). In Christ there is neither male nor female roles: old stereotypes are done away. As Christians we are called to emulate Christ who embodied the best qualities associated with both maleness and femaleness. In his life and ministry this fact is clearly demonstrated.

In Scripture, we have two approaches to the roles of men and women. On the one hand, there is the patriarchal tradition emphasized by the Old Testament writers and the apostles. However, in Ephesians the apostle Paul lifts the status of the woman, as did Christ before him. He not only raised it to that of a *person* (which the rabbis denied), but also to that of equal status with man before God. William Barclay rightly points out that the emphasis in Ephesians is not on "headship," but on "love" (5:22-33).[5]

In teaching that husbands should love their wives as Christ loves the church, Paul called for behavior that was radically different from that practiced by both the Jews and Gentiles of his day. It is difficult for us to appreciate how radical that was. We can only assume that Paul did not advocate complete equality because, as was his practice, he wanted to lead the people one step closer to the ideal of our Lord. We find that he did this with the *slavery* issue. He told the master, Philemon, to receive his slave, Onesimus, back and treat him as a "brother" (Philemon 1:15).

On the other hand, in addition to this modified patriarchal emphasis of the apostles, we have the explicit teaching of our Lord who calls us to play a servant role. Jesus implies that in marriage we are coequals, striving to become one flesh. It is this "new being," the husband and wife in the process of becoming one, that constitutes the head of the family. Christ in turn is the head of the conjugal pair and the family, that is part of his church, his body.

This teaching serves as a corrective to the distorted and exaggerated patriarchal emphasis that many make today. Just as we interpret and evaluate the teachings of the Old Testament in the light of the teachings of Christ, so we must interpret the teachings of the apostles in the light of Christ's teachings.

Having said this, however, each couple must work out an arrangement that is mutually satisfactory. However, any arrangement in which one spouse lords it over the other infringes on that spouse's rights and responsibilities. Such an arrangement is not only detrimental to a marriage, but it is totally unacceptable from a Christian perspective.

Commitment Means Something!

Finally, as Christians we believe that commitment means something! Marriage should be entered with a firm resolve to put love to work in an effort to create oneness. When we said, "I commit myself to you for better or for worse, for richer or for poorer, in sickness and in health," we meant it. Commitment calls for unconditional love.

This enables us to make a commitment that will sustain us during those inevitable periods of hardship, discouragement, sickness, and sorrow which all marriages experience. Marriage with commitment means that when a problem arises, we ask ourselves, "What can I do to resolve it to our *mutual* satisfaction?" not, "How can I get *my* own way?" or "How can *I* escape?"

Changed Behavior

Unfortunately, for many, our family background may not have prepared us for harmonious relationships. We may have come from homes where differences were not peacefully resolved. Or we may be one of those many children who have been pampered and spoiled by overindulgent parents. Or we may have dated extensively, changing dating partners often because we always found things *about them* that we did not like, and never learned to communicate and share.

For these reasons, and many others, some of us must learn new behaviors. When our spouse displays behavior that we do not like (and all of us do), love and caring says, "I will not react in an immature fashion—pout, throw a temper tantrum, give the silent treatment, or walk away. Instead I'll work to develop the habit of walking toward my spouse to work out differences rationally and maturely, building a stronger marriage together."

Changing behavior, not changing partners is the key: communicate, compromise, accommodate and negotiate.

Forget the Past

Those of us who are children of divorce, or have experienced a divorce, must *not* allow negative experiences from the past to cripple our new marriage. Instead, we can learn from the past, and put it behind us. Think Christianly about love, unconditional love, and total commitment. This marriage can and will be a lasting, meaningful one because we have pledged ourselves to put love to work. It is not always the easiest thing to do, but it is the most rewarding and mutually beneficial.

With God's help, and bearing an equal yoke, we can pull together in the same direction to accomplish our mutual goals.

Think It Over

Think it over. Just what is your "religion?" Can you agree on the basic elements of the Christian faith? Have you pledged yourself to the goals of mutual servanthood, and of striving for oneness? If not, consider what changes need to be made to achieve these goals, and begin making them. If you have pledged yourself to these goals, you have taken the first step, a very large step—to a better marriage.

CHAPTER 3

EXPECTATIONS IN MARRIAGE
Adjusting to Reality

It is not uncommon for a wife or a husband who has been married a while to say, "When I got married, I just assumed—

- that we wouldn't have any problems communicating. I expected that we would always be understanding toward one another, and that we would agree on almost everything. I didn't think he would be so stubborn and insist on his own way all the time. I have to do all the giving.

- that love would conquer all. I assumed that the wonderful romantic feelings we felt for each other would continue forever. If he loves me like he says he does, why is he so nasty and disagreeable at times? I thought that love would dissolve all our differences.

- that she would always be affectionate like she was before we got married.

- that sex wouldn't be a hassle. I never dreamed he would be so demanding about sexual intercourse.

- that sex would be spontaneous and fun. I didn't anticipate the *headaches* and comments such as, "Is that all you ever think about?"

- that he wanted children, too.

- that she would take the necessary precautions and not get herself pregnant.

- that when children came she wouldn't get all wrapped in taking care of them and their needs and forget about mine. We never go out much anymore, and when we do, it's always with that kid!
- that money wouldn't be a problem. All she does is spend, spend, spend! She must think that money grows on trees.
- that we would always do things *together*—to the fair, a ball game, a movie, camping, and visiting friends and relatives. We just don't do much together anymore.
- that we would share more leisure time and hobbies together. But the way it has turned out, he does his thing and I do mine. Why, we even have separate television sets!
- that he would be loyal and side with me when his parents and I disagreed. He should be loyal to me, shouldn't he?
- that he would put the family (the children and me) before others. But it seems as though he thinks more about his old buddies than he does of us.
- that he wouldn't fool around with other women after we got married.
- that we would continue to "date" after we got married. But he's so wrapped up in his work, his computer, and other hobbies that he hardly knows I'm around. I never dreamed that he would take me for granted.
- that our faith in God and Christ would be something that we could share together. I never thought he would stop going to church. Before we married he went most of the time. He promised me that we would go together after we were married, but...
- that religion would be a vital part of our family life—you know, grace at meals, and the like.
- that I was marrying her, not her family! I had no idea that she would want to see her parents and grandparents so much. It seems as though we're always at her family's home for holidays.
- that she would stay home and care for the child. I never expected her to put the baby with a sitter and go back to her career six

weeks after the child was born.

- that she would do all the things Mom did for Dad. She expects me to take care of myself. I didn't have to get married for that!

- that she would continue to work and we would be a two paycheck family. I didn't expect her to quit work and stay home with the kid.

- that he would share household responsibilities since both of us are working.

- that she would take some pride in her appearance. I never thought she would let herself go the way she has since we've been married.

- that I was a person in my own right, entitled to my own point of view. Why, he even tries to tell me how to vote!

Do some of these expectations sound familiar to you? No doubt you could add some of your own unrealized expectations to the list above.

There Is Always a "Gap"

It should not come as any surprise that the reality of the marriage experience is different from what we expected. When we went to high school or college the experience was different from what we anticipated.

For that matter, when we stop and think about it, things are seldom what we think they will be. Whether it is joining the church, a service club, or the Peace Corps, whether it is accepting a position with IBM or one as husband or wife in marriage, there is no way of anticipating exactly what it will be like. Even those who try "living together" testify that when they actually got married, "It was different."

A reasonably long courtship prior to marriage, one that is open and honest, enables us to get to know our future spouse fairly well. Nevertheless, all marriages bring with them new experiences and challenges.

The Expectations Gap

Just as we become aware that starting a new job requires adjustments and sacrifices that we did not anticipate, the same is true in marriage. We are not conscious of our expectations immediately. But after a few months have passed, we begin to realize there is a *gap* between our expectations and the reality of our experience. We find our spouse does not react to things as we thought he or she would. But that is to be expected—we married another unique person, not a carbon copy of ourselves. Our spouse was probably just as surprised as we were to find that we didn't measure up to expectations.

It is important to realize that both husbands and wives have these unconscious expectations. All of us experience *the gap*. It's inevitable. It's normal. It's how we react to the differences that is crucial. Acknowledgement of differences is important. Some can be adjusted to and accepted. Others can be negotiated and compromised. Still others can be eliminated. But the only way the gap can be narrowed is through respect for each other, and *each* working to understand the other. It takes work, but then, that's what love is all about.

Narrowing the Gap

The gap between expectations and reality depends on our personality, character, and temperament, as well as on the degree of consensus we share at the outset of marriage. If we share common values, goals, beliefs, and interests, the gap and strain will be less, but one will still exist. It has been our experience, however, that all gaps can be narrowed and we can learn to cope quite well. Successful copers are those who have made a firm commitment to one another.

We believe that the single most important factor that makes for a happy, successful marriage is the conscious commitment on the part of each to make it work. This runs contrary to the spirit of our times. But from a Christian perspective, the institution of marriage (in which two are in the process of becoming one) takes precedence over any notion of unrestricted or absolute personal freedom. Actually, such freedom does not exist. Paradoxically, the more we become one, the greater our personal happiness.

False Expectations

To some extent, all of us develop unrealistic expectations about marriage. We might call these *illusions*, because they are not true. They are based on misconceptions and distortions of reality we pick up as we grow up—from our families, peers, reading, and the mass media. We have a tendency to fantasize about marriage. John F. Crosby says that "illusion is a form of self-deception that enables us to perceive what we wish to perceive and prevents us from perceiving the reality of a situation."[1] Let's look at some of the sources of our false expectations in marriage.

Society's Influence

One source of false expectations is American society in general. Some of the values emphasized are *personal freedom, personal happiness, equality, tolerance for social differences* and *the solvability of all problems.* Many of us are raised on the "American Dream." We are told at home, school, church, and through the mass media, "You can be whatever you want to be!" While these values are worthy ones, we ought not to be naive about reality—not at our age, anyway! We were not all created equal. None of us has unlimited freedom. We cannot be happy, in the ordinary sense of the word, all the time. Happiness is a by-product of responsible living, but often suffering and tragedy strikes the most responsible of people. We know also that some are "more equal" than others. Furthermore, it is one thing to tolerate differences in others outside the family, but quite another when we have to live with someone who has values, beliefs, and life goals that are significantly different from our own. Many problems cannot be solved to everyone's satisfaction. When we do solve them, it often involves compromise. And some invariably have to compromise more than others.

In marriage values create stress and strain because many of our differences have to be adapted to or compromised. Obviously, if in our mate selection we allowed ourselves to be unduly influenced and dominated by romantic love, we may have a larger gap in our marriage than some who proceeded on a more rational basis. Husbands and wives, who came into marriage with different expectations, derived from differences in socioeconomic class, religion, race or ethnic background, values, and life goals, will have to work harder than others. Differences, however, can be enriching to a marriage; they need not pose insurmountable difficulties.

If we overemphasized unconditional personal freedom prior to marriage, then it is only fair that both spouses allow each other considerable freedom within marriage. While we generally find that the responsibilities within marriage require surrendering some freedom, both still need it. Developing skills that demonstrate our commitment to equality, tolerance, and problem solving also enhance our relationship. We are not advocating the abandonment of marital expectations, but merely their modification, so that they fit our new social or corporate experience in marriage.

The Family's Influence

The family in which we were reared is another source of false expectations. Ordinarily we would not think this to be the case. For while we accept the positive traits of our parents readily, we falsely assume that we did not approve of and take on their negative ones. Unfortunately, that's not what actually happens. In reality, we commonly internalize those traits, and find ourselves verbalizing and acting them out in our marriages—the very negative traits we thought we left behind. Much to our surprise and displeasure we find ourselves reacting in these ways when we are under stress.

When you get angry, do you explode or clam up? Do you resemble your dad, your mom, or one of your grandparents? This is not to suggest that we are completely passive in the growing up process and that we don't have a mind of our own. Obviously, we do exercise some discretion in the traits and behaviors we adopt. And it is possible to rise above some destructive aspects of our family and social environment. But such change does not come easily. (How are you coming along with your diet? Your attempt to quit smoking? Your decision to exercise regularly? Or whatever your besetting problem is?) Values, attitudes, and behaviors are *caught*, more than they are taught, and they have a way of clinging to us.

Nevertheless, despite early conditioning within the family, in our marriage we don't have to be held captive by the past. We can draw on other family models that we have observed. In the final analysis we choose what our unique family traits will be. While we were growing up we were able to pick and choose the values, attitudes, and behaviors that we wanted to internalize and practice. And we always have the choice of drawing on the power and grace of God to bring about change in our lives now. We can put love to work—allowing the love of God to make a difference in us.

Much of the difficulty in marriage may stem from a lack of adequate preparation for marriage from our parents. For example, most children receive inadequate sexual education at home. They know little about normal body functions and responses, such as nocturnal emissions or menstruation. What is more, most parents do not allow their own sexual relationship to be revealed in any way to their children. Affection and caring touches are left for the bedroom. The children do not know what is appropriate because they have no models. This is not to say that personal intimacies should be displayed before children. They do need to know, however, that affection is an integral part of marriage.

There are other areas of marital life for which we have no formal training. If we have grown up in traditional homes where male and female roles are firmly established, we will be unprepared if our spouse has a more contemporary view of what is men's or women's work. If communication was poor between parents, we will have poor information about good and appropriate communication. Another example of inadequate preparation for marriage is household finance. More than likely, we were never totally responsible for our financial affairs until after high school or college. For many, the first experience came after marriage. Most families do not include children in household finances except to give them allowances—with little if any guidance about budgeting, tithing, giving, or appropriate and efficient spending. Those who enter marriage poorly prepared invariably experience many difficulties in their relationship, particularly the first few years.

Although the above examples appear to indicate an absence of marital training for children, it does take place. It varies in content and quality from one family to another, but we are instructed by word and example. For example, children learn that affection and touching are either appropriate or inappropriate. Learning takes place even though there was no explicit teaching by the parents, and even though our behavior may not truly reflect our beliefs. Fortunately, much of the training received by children is good. The kinds of skills we need in marriage are the very ones we learned at home. They include such skills as love and consideration for others, the ability to communicate with family members, resolving problems peacefully, sticking with a job until it is done, loyalty, integrity, deferred gratification, self-control, teamwork, honesty, self-denial, self-reliance, trust, and religious faith. These are the very qualities and skills that enable us to put love to work in marriage. We owe a tremendous debt of gratitude to our parents, siblings, relatives, and friends.

For those who have not had the benefits of a stable home, negative teachings can be unlearned through conscious effort—by putting love to work. The characteristics listed above can be cultivated and nurtured to maturity with the strength and assistance God gives to those who ask. Most families, whatever their shortcomings, make some positive contribution to their children's understanding of family responsibility. It may be helpful to identify these in your own lives and to discuss with your spouse how these traits are affecting the quality of your marriage.

Peer Influences

Not only do society and the family contribute to our false expectations about marriage; peers do also. They play a part in the formation of our personality and character, and they influence our values. Beginning in childhood and continuing through early and later adolescence our peers *told* us how to act and think. While we didn't react in robot fashion to their commands, we tended to conform to their expectations. Along with our family, they constituted another reference group from which we took our cues.

We chose our peers—or did they choose us? They dictated to us, and we only slightly modified their prescription. Basically, they supported us in our bid for individualism and freedom from parental control. When it came to dating, especially in adolescence, peers emphasized the physical demonstration of affection. How far we were encouraged to go depended on our peer group. Even with a Christian peer group and the best Christian upbringing, the impact of our permissive society exerted an influence on us.

Adolescence was also a time when we developed interpersonal skills (we learned to relate to others of the same and opposite sex). We learned organizational skills (we planned and carried out leisure and recreational activities). And we learned to "play by the rules" of the group. Some of these skills, as well as others we learned from our peers, we continue to find useful in marriage. But some are not. Recreation and leisure time skills are *not* the most important ones in marriage, although they are more important to us than they were to our parents and grandparents.

Media Influence

In addition to American society, the family, and peers, our expectations are greatly influenced by the mass media, especially

Adjusting to Reality

TV. By the time we married we had been exposed to the full range of TV programming. What kind of values does the media propagate? What expectations have we subconsciously absorbed? For the most part, they are values and behaviors that do not develop stability, harmony, and happiness. With the exception of programs like the *Waltons*, the *Bill Cosby Show*, and *Little House on the Prairie*, TV does not emphasize traditional family values. The message we get is that romantic love and lust is the stuff that male/female relationships are made of—inside and outside of marriage.

For the most part, the message of the media is that "living together" is okay, extramarital sex is normal, divorce (when you are not happy) is an easy way out, children are expendable, and alcohol belongs. Christianity is caricatured in some negative way, but most of the time it is conspicuous by its absence. Self-centeredness is emphasized above all else.

Question: Who's the most important person in the world?
Answer: You are!

Question: What's the chief reason for living?
Answer: To make money!

Question: Why do we need to earn money?
Answer: To have "fun!"

Question: What does fun consist of?
Answer: Sensuous pleasure!

Question: What do you do when "love" is gone?
Answer: Find another person who "turns you on" and move on!

Obviously the message of the media is *not* the Golden Rule, the Great Commandment, the Ten Commandments, or the Sermon on the Mount. It is not total commitment to your wife or husband. It is not unconditional love and responsibility to others—not to mention God. The principles of the Judeo-Christian faith have been replaced by sexual exploitation, self-love, lust, freedom from commitment, violence, war, and the pursuit of pleasure.

It is difficult to live in America and not be influenced by the media. But a healthy marriage cannot be patterned after the soap opera, or the personal lives of movie or television stars. We have been conditioned so long with the self-indulgent, permissive values of the media that it makes a realistic view of marriage and the family difficult. Reality and fantasy mix and become blurred. The answer is to be found in exercising critical judgment. Our Christian expectations and values need to be carefully and consciously extracted from the trash heap of untruths, and clung to, while we discard others.

If we accept the media's view of marriage, we become incredibly disappointed when our spouse fails to act like the leading man or woman of our TV fantasy. The difficulty the media creates becomes evident when fantasy collides with reality. The real world in which we live out our marriages includes working to support a family, maintaining a household, caring for the needs of our spouse and children, relating to friends and kinfolk, coping with sickness, death, and hardship, pursuing some leisure activities, and staying involved in the church and community. If we hope to have a successful Christian marriage, we must reject the selfish, permissive values of the mass media, and follow those values we have forged through experience with God in Christ, the Bible, the family, and the church.

The Women's Rights Movement

The women's rights movement has also influenced our expectations in marriage. The world of today is drastically different from that of our parents and grandparents in every way. Revolutionary advances in science and technology—microchips, computers, robots—have transformed business and industry. Brains and skill have replaced brawn. As we might expect, all these changes have altered our expectations and social behavior. Families are smaller than they were thirty years ago. Today the average family has only one or two children. The mass production and packaging of food and wide variety of household appliances have partially freed women from the drudgery of housework. The time women spend in the kitchen has been cut to a minimum. (Just think for a moment how the microwave oven has revolutionized meal preparation!) The result of all these scientific and technological changes has impacted on the number of women now in the work force. More than four in ten work outside the home.

With the economic emancipation of women, they have become independent and assertive. They do not have to marry for security or "self-fulfillment." When they do marry, they are not willing to settle for a junior partnership anymore. They want equal partnership. Even the churches have interpreted Scripture to teach equality in marriage. Interestingly, studies of conservative Christian couples show that while women verbalize notions of male dominance, they act out their true belief in equality in marriage. Studies also show that both religious and non-religious peoples, who are committed to an equal relationship, or one in which the husband has only slightly more leadership responsibilities, report greater happiness than those who subscribe to a strongly traditional arrangement. As we might expect, these changes in women's attitudes and roles have caused stress and strain in the family, especially with men who have had difficulty adjusting to them.

Men who expected their wives to act toward them as their mothers did toward their fathers have experienced disappointment and frustration. Women who work outside the home have been frustrated, too. They ask, "Why should I be expected to do all the housework after working outside of the home all day? Why shouldn't my husband share in household tasks and child rearing, especially since he benefits from the financial rewards?"

Social and economic changes, primarily in women's roles, have forced men to change and adapt. Unfortunately, many men have not been able or willing to change. Many husbands have reacted negatively to wives who come across too aggressively, overstating their case, and making excessive (or perceived excessive) demands in an attempt to right past wrongs. What is needed in such a situation is not a crusading spirit of confrontation and hostility, but a willingness to sit down and discuss roles and tasks in a spirit of love and mutual respect. This calls for abandoning many false expectations about husband/wife roles and relationships which are now out of date and replacing them with ones that fit the social reality of contemporary society.

False Expectations and the Church

As sociologists actively involved in the church, we are aware of false expectations unintentionally created by ministers and priests in the church. By the very nature of their leadership role, they hold up what they believe to be the Christian ideal in marriage. They talk a great deal about love, caring, self-giving, sacrifice, and kindness—*and rightly so*. They cite the words of our Lord who commands us to strive to be perfect as our Father in heaven is perfect. They tell us to love one another as Jesus loved us.

The result of all this admonition is that we begin to believe that we can actually achieve perfection—that we can live up to the ideal! We develop an image of an ideal mate in an ideal marriage. But when we compare our spouse with the ideal, our partner invariably falls short. We seldom follow the admonition of Robert Burns who suggested that we ask God to give us the ability to see ourselves as others see us.

Of course the church does not deliberately set out to undermine family relations, but this often happens. We become frustrated in trying to live up to the ideal, and find ourselves failing in some ways. Then we repent because we feel somehow we have "failed." We ask our spouse and God to forgive us and help us to live up to the ideal. Then we try and fail again. And on and on it goes. Unfortunately pastors often fail to point out with equal vigor that—since we are finite creatures, who are subject to stress and strain from work, community, and home—*we are going to fail from time to time*. The fact that we are Christians does not exempt us from failure and frustration.

No, don't settle for mediocrity and cast the ideal aside, but allow for a bit of realism and honesty. Keep in mind the fact that ideals are just that—ideals toward which we strive. No one—WE MEAN NO ONE—ever completely lives up to the ideal. We ought not to have unrealistic expectations for our marriage.

The same grace of God that enables us to further develop our virtues can and does enable us to overcome undesirable behaviors. Each of us needs to work at this on our own. It doesn't do any good to point the accusing finger at our spouse. Husbands and wives need to love, pray, forgive, and support their spouse as they seek to meet mutually agreed upon expectations.

To the Remarried

If you are remarried, you have entered this new relationship with definite expectations. You knew the qualities you *did not* want in a spouse this time, as well as those you *did*. This is understandable. It is also a tribute to your intelligence. You have learned from experience. This new marriage need not be a repetition of the previous one, and for most people it isn't. Most second marriages work because the partners have not only learned from experience and chosen a partner with whom they feel more compatible, but because they are more mature and realistic in their expectations.

As you accept the fact that both you and your spouse have differences, celebrate them—make them work to enrich your marriage. Dwell not only on each other's uniqueness, but even more on your common goals, values, and interests. Take the time to learn each others' expectations. Talk about them. Strive to put love to work in meeting them.

Expectations, Reality, and Love

It is inevitable that we enter marriage with false expectations since our experience has been limited to our family, those of relatives, and perhaps a few friends. The values of our society tend to overemphasize personal freedom and self-centeredness. The input from the media and the women's rights movement places a strain on us as we try to sort out who we are and what roles we play in marriage.

We made a point of comparing marriage to other new experiences we embarked on, such as taking a job and finding that the actual experience on the job was different from what we had anticipated. When this happened, we adjusted our expectations and abandoned false ones and developed new ones. We changed our behavior and attitudes. We made the best of it. We coped and found it rewarding.

So in most cases with marriage, the key to greater happiness is not to "quit," or abandon all expectations, but to change and adapt to the reality of the situation. Since both husband and wife come with expectations, both need to modify them. It's fruitless to spend time finding fault, complaining, and blaming the other partner for not measuring up to our expectations. It is more rewarding to discuss each of your expectations for your marrage *now,* and then each put love to work meeting them. This requires humility and effort on the part of both spouses, but the outcome is worth it!

This is no easy task. We dare not allow foolish pride to get in the way. We must admit to ourselves, as well as to our spouse, that we want to change, that we want to know ways in which we failed to do things they would like us to do, as well as things they would like to see *us* stop doing. Avoid becoming defensive; resist the temptation to rationalize and justify present unacceptable behaviors. Demonstrate a degree of maturity and courage—perhaps more than you have been willing to invest in your marriage before.

But we are talking about enhancing relationships with the one we love. We have made a lifetime commitment to one another. Our mutual goals are to build up one another in love, to support and encourage each other, and to facilitate marital happiness.

Adjusting to Reality

The best way for us to embark on a course of improving our marriage is for each individual to work to change his or her *own* behavior. Quiet times of meditation and prayer are helpful in this process—tremendously helpful. If we get alone with God, he can and will show us ways we can change and improve. One way we can do this is by reading God's Word, the Scriptures. As we read the Bible, God's Spirit helps us to apply the Word to our personal and family life. Through prayer, God helps us to see ourselves not only as others see us, but as he sees us. And God enables us to humble ourselves. He helps us to see what we can become, and he gives us the power to change ourselves into that person. Prayer is God's gift to us—not to bend his will to ours, but our wills to his.

The Christian ideal is not "me first," but God and others first. As we obey the teachings of our Lord we can grow, and find greater happiness—personally and in our marriage. Jesus calls us to self-denial. But paradoxically, it is when we obey our Lord, deny ourselves, and take up our cross and follow him that we *all* end up winners!

CHAPTER 4

LOVE IN MARRIAGE
A Way of Behaving

Love is the greatest force in the world—and it is with us! Regrettably, for various reasons we do not use it as much as we could. Putting love to work takes effort, but the fruit of our efforts will enrich our marriage and family life beyond all expectations. It will transform the most frustrating and unhappy situations into ones that are peaceful and enjoyable.

God created us in love so that we could not only love him with all our heart, soul, mind, and strength, but also so that we could love others and ourselves. Our capacity to love is derived from God. We are born with the desire to love and be loved. The ability to love is nurtured in our social environment, especially in the family. But regardless of the opportunities we have had to learn healthy expressions of love in our family, anytime we are ready we can further develop and improve our capacity to love. We can turn our lives around by saying "yes" to love!

God models love for us. We experience it in Jesus Christ, the one *in* and *through* whom God's grace is revealed. As Christians, God's love fills our hearts by his indwelling Holy Spirit. Through the power of the Spirit we also are strengthened to do God's will. Furthermore, the Spirit enables us to discipline our lives, to do acts of love, and to speak words that are kind and helpful.

Meaning of Love

Because the word *love* is abused so much, we thought it

might be better to substitute another word for affection and its expression. When we love everything from cotton candy to God, its meaning becomes clouded. A word like "care" might keep the meaning from being trivialized. But no doubt people would corrupt "care" as they have "love." So we will stick with love and define it carefully.

Most truth seems to possess contradictory qualities and characteristics. And love is no exception. Love is indeed "a many-splendored thing"—it has many facets. Elizabeth Barrett Browning tried to convey this in her beautiful poem, "How do I love thee, let me count the ways...." The ways we love are indeed varied and so are the emotions associated with it.

Love Is Not an Emotion

It may be helpful first of all to clarify what love is not.[1] Love is generally classified as an emotion. This is questionable, although emotions are involved in loving. Emotions are also involved when we hate. They are involved in everything we do. We are emotional beings, as well as rational ones. The difference between the emotions of love and hate generally lies in that which is being *willed*. In love we *will* the well-being of another; we *act* to enhance another's life. When we hate, we *will* and we *act* to demean and destroy another. Pleasing emotions result from positive thoughts, words, and actions. When thoughts, words, and actions are negative we experience hostile and destructive feelings. But when love is "tough," when it confronts and challenges others who are acting unjustly or unlovingly, the euphoric feeling is absent. Love often "hurts" the parties involved.

More Than a Romantic High

Contrary to what most adolescents and older romantics believe, authentic love is not some blind, indescribable force that zaps us. There is no Cupid who shoots "love arrows" into our hearts and throws us into a tizzy, making us see stars, and causing us to walk on clouds. Loss of appetite and increased levels of adrenalin are no indication of genuine love.

Nor is love something we fall into or out of, as one falls into or out of bed. There are identifiable reasons why love flourishes or dies. It must be nourished to grow. When a woman says, "I don't love my husband anymore," it's not a conclusion she arrived at overnight.

Take the case of Jane and Russ, for example. Jane said, "I don't love Russ anymore. I'm ready to divorce him!" When asked why, she is very specific in her reasons. She says, "He takes me for granted. He does not come home for meals on time. He never has time for me or the children. He's dumped all the responsibility for rearing them on me. I have to drive them to little league, to music lessons, to wherever they need to go. Besides, he drinks too much and gets abusive, loses his temper, and pushes me around." She paused and then added, "How's that for starters!"

Obviously, the sense of alienation Jane feels for Russ is not something that happened overnight. It has been developing over a long period of time. Jane was pushed out of a good relationship by Russ's failure to act responsibly. He was thoughtless and inconsiderate. She had had enough. When he refused to come in for counseling, and began to physically abuse her and the children, she picked them up and left.

Jane did not suddenly fall out of love. Russ no longer talked or acted in a loving manner. Jane concluded that he no longer loved her because there was no *evidence* of love. Was she wrong?

If relationships within marriage become strained, we don't have to look far for the answer. Stop and ask, "When did I notice that our relationship began to become strained? What was I thinking? What was *I doing* and *saying* that contributed to this alienation between us?" Don't waste time blaming your spouse. You can't change another person unless that person wants to change. We can only change ourselves—our behavior. In many cases, if *we* change, this will cause a change in our spouse.

Studies show that when people change their behavior toward a person, their attitudes and feelings also change. This is true of husbands and wives also. We can choose to change the way we use our time and resources. We can change destructive thoughts and actions to constructive ones. When we change, our feelings toward the other person will change and harmony will be restored and growth will occur in our marriage.

Realistically, we cannot sustain the romantic feelings associated with courtship. As one writer put it: "The euphoric state most of us experience during courtship is a temporary one which our culture prepares us for and thrusts upon us. The tragedy is that we believe that state can be sustained. In reality, once married, the pressures and demands of 'life' reappear, and the time and effort that was concentrated in courtship is dissipated over the other areas of personal life. This is not to say that one should not work to retain 'romance' in marriage, but to point to the fact that it does require a concerted effort on the part of both spouses to keep the lines of communication open and harmony in marriage. Growth of a cultivated flower takes 'work'—only thistles and 'stink weeds' grow *naturally*."[2]

But while romantic love cannot be maintained at the same fever pitch we may have experienced in courtship, idealization is vital to a good marriage. We still need some romance, no matter how long we have been married. We should treat our spouses courteously, realizing just how special they are and how fulfilling they make life for us.

In *My Fair Lady*, Eliza says to Mr. Higgins, "He (Colonel Pickering) always showed me that he felt and thought about me as if I were something better than a common flower girl. You see, Mr. Higgins, apart from the things one can pick up, the difference between a lady and a flower girl is not how she behaves, but how she is treated. I shall always be a flower girl to Professor Higgins because he always treats me as a flower girl and always will. But I know that I shall always be a lady to Colonel Pickering because he always treats me as a lady, and always will."

It's a fact! We get what we give. If we respect our wife as a beautiful person, and consider ourselves fortunate to be married to her, then we will show our gratitude by what we say and do. But if we think she is mighty lucky to have captured such a gorgeous "hunk," and if we think *she* married up while *we* married down, then this will be evident in the way we treat her. The same is true of a wife's assumptions and behaviors toward her husband.

Think for a few moments of those characteristics of your spouse that are very special to you. Then share these with your spouse as a way of showing gratitude. Thank God for the good qualities you bring to each other.

An Unconditional Commitment

Love, then, is more than an emotion, and more than a romantic high. Grammatically, love is used both as a *noun* and as a *verb* (yes, and as an adjective and an adverb). Used as a noun, love is defined by one dictionary as "unselfish concern that freely accepts another in loyalty and seeks his (or her) good." This definition has several important components. First, love involves *self-giving*—unselfish concern for another. Second, it involves *freedom of will*—we freely accept another in love. Third, it involves *total commitment*—loyalty. Fourth, it involves *working* for the good of another—one seeks another's well-being.

When we marry we make a *love-commitment* to our spouse. Love in marriage must be unconditional. This kind of commitment is necessary for a marriage to last. We give our word to stay with our spouse "for better or for worse, for richer or for poorer, in sickness and in health." We also promise to forsake all others, and remain loyal and faithful to our partner "so long as we both shall live." To maximize our happiness, this commitment of unconditional love needs to be mutual. (It is helpful to reflect on these promises. Birthdays, Valentine's Day, and anniversaries give us opportunities to do just that!)

This commitment of unconditional love is the solid rock foundation on which good marriages are built. When our spouse or child is ill, when death and tragedy strike, when we lose a job, when we experience periods of stress, when we feel bored with it all and wish we could just walk away, our wife or husband needs the assurance that we will still love and be there.

The strength we derive from this unconditional commitment of total acceptance results in a reservoir of love that overflows to others. Just as experiencing God's redemptive love through Jesus Christ on a daily basis enables us to love others, so the daily experience of unconditional love from our spouse and children increases our ability to extend love to others.

An Active State of Being

Love is also used as an "active verb." Loving behavior incorporates not only the way we *think*, but also the way we speak and act. It includes all that we do to maximize the health and well-being of others. As a by-product of *being* a loving person we also enhance our own well-being.

Love is not merely an active verb, it is a transitive verb. It takes an object. The proper object of love is not things we create or something in the natural world, but persons. To love things or material objects is a waste. It is a form of idolatry. We are only to love God and human beings. God cautions us not to worship idols, for they not only give us a distorted notion of reality, but also destroy the soul.

Love Can Grow

Since we are free to exercise our will, we can increase or strengthen our love for another. We can accomplish this by consciously doing things that please our loved one. By identifying the situations in which we act out of self-centeredness rather than other-centeredness, we can clearly see the areas in which love has the potential to grow.

For example, in families where the wife is at home all day, the husband's daily homecoming is often met with a massive dose of conversation, questions, and even complaints. Because the wife has been confined to the home all day with little adult social interaction, she is probably not thinking about what kind of a day her husband had. Allowing a few quiet moments before assaulting him with the day's problems demonstrates a move from a self-centered perspective to an other-centered one. It opens the door for love to grow.

The events in the wife's day are important and should be shared—but only after the husband has had a few moments to collect his thoughts and relax.

Love's Many Expressions

Some writers spend a good bit of time identifying different words for love, each word conveying a specific type of love and the person(s) to whom it applies. The Greek words *agape, storge, philia,* and *eros* are associated with self-giving, family, friendship, and sensuous love, respectively.

An Asian Indian colleague, Dr. Renuka Biswas, tells us that in Indian literature and scripture the following words are used for love: *batsalya* (love of parents or older persons), *dasya* (love for a superior), *bhakti* (love for the deity), *prem* (sensual love), *sakhya* (love for a friend), and *parakia/prem* (platonic love, as well as illicit love).

In English, however, we have only one word for love. We use an adjective to designate the kind of love we are talking about—for example, "romantic love." While using one word to convey the idea of love has its liabilities, we think it also has an advantage: love is love is love. There are not, in reality, different kinds of love, but one love (caring) that we express in different ways. We show our love for God in reverent worship, by doing justice, and by showing kindness to others. We show our love for our wives or husbands by treating them as equals, caring and ministering to their needs, and by granting them complete freedom to maximize their own potential. We love our children by providing for them, protecting and nurturing them, and by gradually allowing them to mature into independent adults. We love our friends by sharing and caring for them, through mutual respect and trust.

A Way of Behaving

All of these ways of thinking, speaking, and acting are expressions of love through which we help others to maximize their potential. By living in this self-giving way we also find fulfillment ourselves. But we do not do for others what they can and should do for themselves.

Words and Deeds

While behavior expresses our love, obviously not all words or acts are manifestations of love. Not only our intention, but the social context of the situation and the psychological/spiritual condition of the recipient of our words or deeds determine whether they are received as messages of love.

When one of the authors was in graduate school with his wife, their apartment was next to a couple who often had rather loud arguments. The walls between the apartments were thin. When they argued, it was almost as if we were in their apartment! The interesting thing about their verbal exchanges was that they would continue to use endearing terms, even though they were going at each other tooth and claw. He would yell with a snarl, "Well, darling...!" and she would "affectionately" respond, "Well, sweetheart...!" The tone and volume clearly conveyed hostility, not love.

Acts popularly associated with love are also not necessarily so. For example, sexual intercourse, when not mutually desired, becomes a selfish act. Or worse, a case of rape in marriage! The degree and quality of communication is important in determining whether words and actions will be interpreted as love, hate, hostility, or rejection.

The Scripture clearly teaches that our profession of love for God is validated by just, holy, and righteous living. In a similar way, our profession of love for our wife or husband is supported by loving behavior that confirms our profession. The prophet Micah, in the 8th century before Christ, wrote (italics mine): "He has showed you, O man, what is good. And what does the Lord require of you? To *act* justly and to *love* mercy and to *walk* humbly with your God" (6:8). We show our love for God when we walk humbly with him and when we love others, beginning with God then with our spouse and children and then with others. The emphasis is on *behavior*! Merely mouthing platitudes such as "I love you" is not enough. Profession and practice must be simultaneous.

Interestingly, Jesus clearly taught that mercy, forgiveness, compassion, and selfless living are the marks of love and authentic discipleship. And this begins with our *closest neighbors*—those in our family!

Measuring Love

When we think about love in relation to marriage and the family, it is helpful if we *operationally define* the word. That is, if we define it so that we can measure it to see if indeed we are loving. There is no better criteria set forth to measure love than those given by the apostle Paul in his first letter to the Christians at Corinth. Here is Paul's classic "operational definition" of love:

> This love of which I speak is
>   slow to lose patience—
> It looks for a way of being constructive.
> It is not possessive:
> It is neither anxious to impress
>   nor does it cherish inflated ideas of
> Its own importance.
> Love has good manners
>   and does not pursue selfish advantage.
> It is not touchy.
> It does not keep account of evil
>   or gloat over the wickedness of other people.
> On the contrary, it is glad with all
>   good men when truth prevails.
> Love knows no limit to its endurance,
>   no end to its trust,
>   no fading of its hope;
>   it can outlast anything.
> It is, in fact, the one thing that still stands when all else has fallen.
>   (1 Corinthians 13:4—8a, Phillips)

Now it is amazing how many of these characteristics of love couples actually identify. Over the past several years one of the authors asked men and women what attributes and/or behaviors they associate with love. Here are the most common qualities mentioned:

Acceptance—not trying to change your partner
Affection—not unfeeling, cold, or distant
Caring—not unconcerned or indifferent; caring enough to confront your partner with issues disruptive to the relationship
Emphatic and understanding—not prejudging or condemning
Fidelity—not unfaithful
Forgiving—not holding grudges
Honest—not deceitful or lying
Humility—not arrogant, proud
Open communication—not disregarding the opinions and views of others
Overlook faults—not hypercritical, faultfinding
Respect—not rude and disrespectful
Sacrificial/sharing—not selfish
Thoughtful—not inconsiderate or ill-mannered
Trusting—not jealous
Total commitment—no reservations

No doubt you could add other criteria of mature love. Often in a group session couples list negative traits that are *not* signs of love—similar to those listed to the right of the attributes of love above. Interestingly, couples seldom mention sex when thinking of the attributes of love. It isn't that they don't think it is important, but they usually say that it is the inevitable result of good communication in a loving relationship.

Wisdom in Marriage

In any discussion of love and how to put it to work, mention of wisdom is helpful. We need wisdom to know *how* and *when* to speak or to refrain from speaking, and when to act or not act. If the timing is off, if the wrong words are spoken, if the behavior is inappropriate, it will not be received as an act of love. The apostle James tells us that wisdom can be ours if we but ask God who freely grants it. He also wisely counsels us to be "*quick* to listen, *slow* to speak and *slow* to become angry" (1:19).

If we can avoid acting or speaking in anger, or too hastily, we are better off. We all know that. The trick is in doing it! Remember the Golden Rule. If we think about how we would like our wife or husband to speak or act toward us in a situation, we will probably respond more wisely and lovingly.

Rather than criticizing, find ways to be supportive and encouraging. When a spouse is fearful of facing a given task, reassurance is not only needed but greatly appreciated. "You can do it, honey! You've got the intelligence and ability. Give it a try. I know you'll do a good job!" Words of encouragement that convey confidence are not only an expression of love, but they strengthen our spouse's self-image.

At times we almost intuitively know what we ought to do. For example, one couple shared the experience of celebrating their anniversary. Both worked outside the home full time. The wife's idea of a perfect celebration was to dine out. She could return home at the end of the day, not saddled with the responsibility of preparing a meal and having to clean up following an already tiring day. For the husband, the ideal was different. He preferred having a special dinner at home, away from the noise and distraction of other people. He wanted peace, quiet, and privacy, as well as a home-cooked meal. The wife decided that she wanted to express her love for her husband by foregoing her own comfort and giving of her time in order that her husband might have the experience he preferred.

Some people say, "If I were her, I wouldn't let him get away with that. He should be more sensitive and loving toward her. After all, she did all the work." While it's true there could have been a compromise and the husband could have prepared or helped to prepare the meal, that is not the point. Out of love, she chose to give him what he desired. (On the other hand, he could have forgone his preference out of love for his wife, without putting pressure on her to celebrate at home.)

There are times when we do things for one another just because we love one another. When we love someone we go the second and third mile, not just because it pleases others, but also because it is good for us.

On the other hand, there are times when we *should not* do things for the one we love. Each of us needs to strengthen our sense of self-worth. We need to mature, to become independent and self-reliant. To accomplish this, each of us has to bear our own responsibility, carry our own load. For example, a husband may be shy and ill at ease in social situations and feel that he must have his wife along to do his speaking for him. Although the wife may believe that interacting with others is helpful and loving, she may actually be preventing her husband's growth and maturity. In the long run, the kinder behavior would be to give her shy husband some pointers about socializing and let him go into these situations himself. Eventually, he will be able to speak for himself and be a better person for it.

But in addition to carrying our own weight, we must do things for others. By *doing* we develop a feeling of self-worth. It is no accident that Jesus' Beatitudes all begin with the phrase, "*Blessed* [or *Happy*] *is* . . ." the person who embraces attitudes, values, and behaviors that are just and compassionate and make for peace. Acting in a self-giving manner *is* the key to personal happiness. Therefore, when we do anything that robs our wives or husbands of the experiences that make for self-fulfillment, we are *not* putting love to work. We are being selfish. We are robbing them of a chance to grow!

Furthermore, there are times when wisdom tells us that love means letting our spouse alone. We all need privacy—our own space. We need time to reflect, to talk to God, to talk to ourselves, and we sometimes need time just to putter around for a while.

Confronting in Love

There are times, also, when love means caring enough to confront your partner with those behaviors, attitudes, and words that we find offensive and disturbing. This is a touchy area to handle. Scripture admonishes us to "speak the truth in love." But try as we may to do this, there is no way our wife or husband will not feel some hurt when we confront. Again, timing is important.

Love, however, that thinks in terms of the *long run*, instead of the *short run*, makes a spouse aware of the offending behavior. While in the short run failing to confront may avoid the unpleasantness that invariably results, in the long run failure to do so will broaden the gap between a couple. We must realize that the *apparent* peace and harmony that prevails is just that—a false peace. Yet the apostle Peter reminds us that love overlooks a multitude of sins or shortcomings—and each of us has them. None of us models perfection for our spouse! Since our partner puts up with our faults and idiosyncrasies, shouldn't we tolerate or, better still, accept behaviors that are not necessarily wrong, but merely a matter of personal preference or uniqueness?

On one occasion psychiatrist Lynnwood Hopple was discussing the causes of marital dissatisfaction and conflict. Dr. Hopple drew a circle on a large piece of white paper, like the one below.

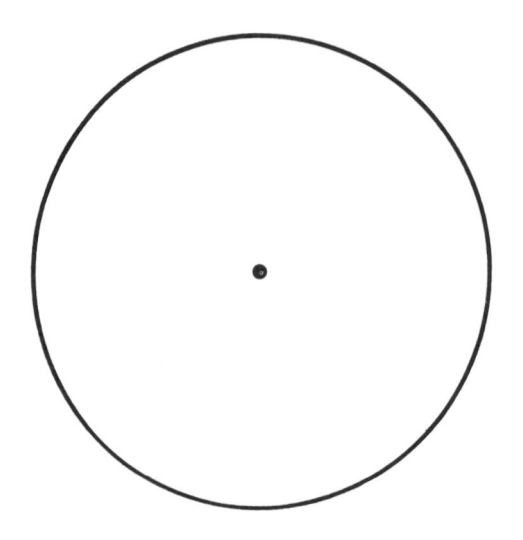

Then he asked the group, "What do you see?"

"A large circle with a black dot in the middle of it," someone replied.

"You're right; most people do see the dot," he answered. "But actually, the largest space in the circle is white. In marriage," he continued, "too often we dwell on the few 'dots' or shortcomings of our mates, rather than praising or celebrating their many virtues."

Dr. Hopple is obviously right. We can be a fault-finding, self-righteous individual—looking past the log in our own eye to get at the splinter of wood in our spouse's eye. Or we can be a grateful, appreciative lover who celebrates our wife's or husband's virtues, thereby strengthening our marriage.

Love Is Patient

It is also important to show our love through patience. Think about it. When we come to God, he accepts us as we are (but he does not leave us the way we were). God does not demand that we transform ourselves into saints overnight. If God did, he would be the most disappointed person in the universe. God has infinite patience! How long has it taken us to change some of our offensive traits? So, God says to us, "Be patient, forgiving one another, as I have forgiven you in Christ." Similarly, we should accept our spouse as he or she is. As each of us puts love to work in our relationships, God will use that, among other things, as a way of bringing about change.

For example, a husband had quite a lengthy list of positive characteristics. But one of them was *not* consistency. Any task that required daily attention was difficult for him. The couple had a dehumidifier in the basement that ran only at night. It had to be turned on before bedtime, and turned off and emptied in the morning. The husband chose to take on the task. Many evenings the dehumidifier was not turned on and the basement remained damp. But the wife remained uncritical and supportive—even though, at times, she felt like screaming. She praised him freely when the job was well done. After six months, rarely a night went by that the dehumidifier did not run. Patience and love were the key to success. Obviously, this situation generated love for both spouses, even though it was such a simple matter.

A Helpful Exercise

We can help put love to work by engaging in *role reversal*. A husband should put himself in his wife's place and think about all he has said and done, as well as what he has failed to do and say. If he does this, he will soon realize that he has not done all that he could to facilitate her growth. The same is true for the wife.

Periodic role reversal, meditation, and reflection can really lead to greater empathy and insight into ways that we can make progress in our marriages. It will help us face up to our own weaknesses. While role reversal is painful, it is one technique that God can use to give us insight into the ways we can put love to work effectively.

Expressing Love

While love is behavior, it is important to observe that not all people express love in the same ways. Some men, for example, show their love by working at two jobs, bringing home extra money for the wife and family. Some women show their affection through their excellent culinary skills. Some verbalize affection. Others enjoy receiving and giving physical expression of their love. Judson Swihart makes the point that we need to analyze the ways each partner shows affection in marriage.[3] By doing this we can better understand and appreciate the messages of love we send each other. But perhaps even more important, we need to know whether these ways of loving are the ones that are most meaningful to our spouse. If it is more time together she wants, then a fatter pay check is a poor substitute. If he enjoys physical intimacy, then gourmet cooking will scarcely meet the need. How do you want to be loved? Tell your spouse. Spouses are not mind readers.

If the ways we are saying "I love you" are not the ways our wife or husband appreciate wouldn't it be best if we changed? Unless love is conveyed in a mutually acceptable fashion, we cannot make a satisfactory adjustment in marriage. And if we fail in our adjustment with our spouse, then the entire family suffers.

Love Is Reciprocal

Expressions of loving behavior are not necessarily simultaneous. As Lenore and Richard Kintzing (who have been happily married for over fifty years) said, "Love is reciprocal." We often alternate and reciprocate in our expressions of love. A husband will do something for her because he loves her, and then she will do something for him because she loves him. Love moves us to do things for one another because we care, not because we necessarily enjoy doing it. The thing that makes the deed an act of love is that it pleases our spouse. A wife may not like to iron, especially shirts. She does it, however, because she loves him and likes to see him well dressed. She knows that he does not like to paint trim around the house, but he does it because it pleases her (and because it preserves their property value). And there are other areas of our relationship where we reciprocate. Pop psychology is not helpful that tells us, "Don't do anything you don't want to do! Be your own person!" Such notions tend to become a license for selfishness and narcissism—not love.

Love May Include Conflict

Love does not mean absence of conflict. "Perfect love" is an ideal toward which we strive, but one which we can never fully attain. God is the only one who loves us perfectly. The apostle Paul indirectly acknowledged the virtual impossibility of loving perfectly. In his practical counsel to the Christians at Rome he told them to do everything possible on their part to live in peace with everybody (Roman 12:18). While this is difficult to do, Paul urges us to try anyway.

Husbands and wives often fault one another when conflict

arises or when their partner disappoints them in one way or another. "You yell at me like that, and yet you say you love me, George!" "Alice, you come home late like this and now we have to miss that dinner party. Yet you say you love me!" And the clincher, "Well, then, you didn't mean a thing you said last night, did you!" To attack your spouse with statements such as these is unjust and a bit cruel. We all say (or fail to say), do (or fail to do) things that may not be positive and constructive.

Many times the pressures of family life, finances, the job, health problems, and social duties impinge on us and we say and do things that we ordinarily would not. At those times we are really "not ourselves." Conflict and misunderstandings are inevitable if we are married to another living human being! This is not to excuse unloving words or actions, but we must realize that lapses do occur. For growing persons are always in the process of becoming. Life is complex. We are relating not only to our spouse, but to our children, parents, in-laws, employers, co-workers, friends, and others. The larger our circle of relationships, the greater the possibility for tension and stress. Trouble in one area of life spills over into another—especially at home.

The old song is unfortunately true, "You always hurt the ones you love, the ones you shouldn't hurt at all." This is why unconditional commitment is necessary as the rock foundation on which we build. Then when times of stress and unpleasantness occur we need not fear that our spouse will desert us, nor will we ascribe too much weight to them.

It's on occasions when our wives, husbands, or children have a bad day, that they need our understanding, empathy, support, and encouragement the most. Sometimes silence is the best response. Love that overlooks a multitude of faults goes a long way toward maintaining harmonious relationships.

Love of Self

Although we have defined love as unselfishness and caring for others, there is an element in all our relationships that has to do with love of self. This is not a self-centered form of love, but a genuine liking of oneself. It is accepting oneself as one is, the good and the bad.

While the "good" is accepted with pleasure and satisfaction, we need to see the "bad" as a challenge for change. Self-love is recognizing that God has created us in *his* image. He values us highly—higher than any other part of his creation. Scripture affirms this fact. We are his and he loves us no matter what condition or circumstance we find ourselves in.

The results of self-hatred, or disliking oneself, can be devastating to one's own life, as well as to the lives of others. Having a poor self-image and low self-esteem often has dire consequences. We may think that the world, including our spouse, is "out to get us."[3] If we believe our spouse is deliberately trying to harm us, we will respond in a defensive manner. Communication will be impeded. We may simply be afraid to share openly. We may believe our feelings are faulty or invalid, or that our spouse will not understand, or will laugh at us. We may fail to be assertive, allowing ourselves to become a doormat for others. Because we feel "stupid" we may believe that we cannot change. We may bear a heavy burden of guilt, and we may expect bad things to happen to us because we think we deserve them. If we believe that we are unattractive, unlovely, and unlovable, our sexual relations may be seriously impaired.

But there is good news. We *are* in control of the feelings we have about ourselves. If we find that feelings of self-hatred and unconstructive behavior are preventing us from good marital relationships, it's helpful to remember that God created us and loves us unconditionally. Therefore, there is no reason we ought not to love ourselves. As the apostle Paul said, "If God is for us, who can be against us?" (Romans 8:31). Jesus, himself, reminds us that we should love ourselves (Mark 12:31). It is healthy to say, "I am me, and I am okay." Having a good self-image and healthy self-esteem opens up the way for us to live up to our full potential as a person, a spouse, and as a parent.[4]

Four Relationships

Our love benefits us most when it is directed in at least four ways—to God, our spouse, our family, and others in the community. Because there are so many people toward whom we wish to express our love, and because of our limited time and resources, we often feel frustrated and stressful. There are times in the marriage and family life cycle when we must concentrate our attention on someone with special needs. For example, when a new baby arrives, infant and child care take a lot of time. The teenage years of children are stressful for most parents. Sometimes aging parents and grandparents use up our time. As mature adults we try to be supportive and understanding, and not become jealous of those who usurp our spouse's time.

Because of the need to keep things in proper perspective, our priorities need to be straight. Life will run more smoothly when God is kept in first place. Why? Because communication with God through Scripture, prayer, and meditation provides the principles and guidance and dynamic we need to relate to others.

Next in order, is giving priority to the love relationship with our wife or husband. Moses, Jesus, and Paul all remind us that our primary allegiance in the family is to our wife or husband—not our children, parents, in-laws, work, civic club, golf, or TV. This bond of mutual love provides the security that enables us to fulfill our other obligations to love. Furthermore, it gives the children the security they need.

Third comes love for our children. A caution is in order here. When we find it difficult communicating with our spouse, we should not identify with our children and look to them for the love and security that should normally come from our spouse. Children are not psychologically able to handle it. Children are just that—children. We need to face up to our problems with our spouse and confront each other in love. Talk things out. Children need two parents who can give them the love and guidance they need—and they do need it. As they pass through the various stages of the life cycle they make varied demands upon us. We only have so much time and energy. During these growing years parents need to make adjustments for them. Mature parents face this task together, putting love to work as we hand more and more responsibility over to them.

Fourth, we have obligations to the larger community and the church. There are needy people out there who deserve our assistance. We are our brother's and sister's helper. To fail to give time, money, and self is to renege on our humanity, not to mention our Christian calling.

Finally, love will flourish best when we individually sustain an active religious life that includes both private and corporate worship. Religious involvement is not an option that we can omit without tremendous loss to self, family, and community. We are spiritual beings, as well as physical beings. We are members of the body of Christ, his church. There is an eternal dimension to our personality and existence. Our spiritual relationship with God through Christ and the Spirit affects every other aspect of our personal and social life. It will continue beyond the grave. God must be our first love—loving him with all our heart, soul, mind, and strength. Only in this way can we be sure that we will love others fully and properly.

Begin the day with a petition to God. Ask God to help you do and say those things that will make the lives of your wife/husband/child/family, and associates richer and fuller. If you do this, you will certainly be starting off on the right track. Love is the greatest force in the world, and it is with you!

Shakespeare's Sonnet 116
Let me not to the marriage of true minds
Admit impediments. Love is not love
Which alters when it alteration finds,
Or bends with the remover to remove.
Oh, no! it is an ever-fixed mark
That looks on tempests and is never shaken;
It is the star to every wandering bark,
Whose worth's unknown, although its height be taken.
Love's not Time's fool, though rosy lips and cheeks

Within his bending sickle's compass come;
Love alters not with his brief hours and weeks,
But bears it out even to the edge of doom.
If this be error and upon me prov'd,
I never writ, nor no man ever lov'd.

CHAPTER 5

COMMUNICATION IN MARRIAGE
The Key to Growth and Happiness

Virtually all marriage counselors say that good communication is a key to successful marital adjustment—if not *the* key.

Communication goes on all the time, whether we want it to or not! Even silence speaks loudly at times. We communicate by word, gesture, facial expression, tone, and loudness of voice. Sven Wahbroos defines communication as "any behavior that carries a message which is perceived by someone else. The behavior can be verbal or nonverbal; it is still communication as long as it carries a message. The message may be intended or unintended, but if it is perceived, it has, in fact, been communication. The perception of the message may be conscious or unconscious, distorted or undistorted; but as soon as the message gets through on any level, we have communication."[1]

Since we cannot avoid communication, it is in the best interest of the wife or husband to put love to work improving communication skills. Good communication leads to understanding, understanding to increased knowledge and acceptance, and all of these to mutual respect and a well-adjusted relationship in marriage.

Basic and Nonbasic Conflict

Before we turn to the subject of communication, let us

briefly discuss basic and nonbasic conflict and the important question of the power structure in marriage. The power structure definitely affects both marital relationships and the content and style of communication. John Scanzoni identifies four possible relationships between husband and wife.[2]

1. *Owner/Property:* The husband has rights: the wife has duties.
2. *Head/Complement:* The husband is more powerful than the wife. While she is still submissive, she has limited freedom to participate in community activities.
3. *Senior Partner/Junior Partner:* The wife works outside the home and gains more power, status, and independence.
4. *Equal Partner/Equal Partner:* Husband and wife have interchangeable roles and equal power in decision making.

Couples invariably select one of these power structures. Lack of agreement on the structure generates *basic conflict*—disagreement over the basic rules of the game in marriage. Nonbasic conflict centers around disagreements within the rules. For example, a couple may be operating as equals in category 4. When a decision must be made concerning the kind of home to buy, both will have equal say in the process of choosing. But there may be disagreement over what type of house to buy, and how it will be furnished. The wife may decide that it should be her decision. Since she seems to do more of the decorating and managing of the household, she attempts to change the basic rules and operate in category 3 with herself as the senior partner.

It is important that a couple agree on the basic power structure that will prevail in their marriage. It is helpful to agree on *who* will play *what roles* and on what goals the couple are striving to achieve. While we are free to select our roles, and these may be interchangeable, the power structure is a decision that should be mutual and fixed. At least it should be firm, until *both* agree to change it.

In reference to the four options each couple has, the Owner/Property relationship is clearly unacceptable and inconsistent with Christian principles (although there are people who still live in this type of a relationship). Most American marriages fit into the Head/Complement or the Senior Partner/Junior Partner arrangement, with the Equal Partner pattern growing in popularity. The authority structure reflected in some of Paul's writings seem to emphasize 2 and 3, while other Scripture lend support to the Equal Partner relationship which I have chosen to call one of *mutual servanthood* (Ephesians 5:21-33; Colossians 3:18-19; 1 Timothy 2:9-15; Mark 10:42-45; Luke 22:24-27; Matthew 20:25-28). However, a husband and wife must decide which relationship they feel most comfortable with. It is a matter for each couple to decide. We all know excellent families that fit into 2, 3, or 4. Once a couple select their basic relationship, and abide by it, basic conflict is reduced or virtually eliminated, and communication is made much easier.

Nonbasic conflict will continue, however, for it is a vital part of a good marriage. It continues because both the husband and wife grew up in different family subcultures. They participated in families that exposed them to unique male and female roles. They were exposed to different experiences and opportunities in chilhood and adolescence and emerged as unique individuals. Therefore, each brings into marriage their concept of what the roles of a husband and a wife should be. In their own marriage the process of change and adaptation will continue.

For example, when a boy and a girl hear the word fast, different thoughts run through their minds. On the one hand, a young boy may think of a fast car or of running faster than the other boys or the girls on the soccer team. He wants to impress the coach, his family, and others, particularly the girls, because he has come to believe it is important for boys to have athletic ability. On the other hand, a young girl may be warned by her parents to stay away from the "fast crowd" to guard her reputation. To the boy, the word *fast* had a positive meaning; to the girl, *fast* has a negative connotation. By the time the boy enters high school, however, the word *fast* takes on a sexual connotation also. This is just one illustration of the fact that males and females are culturally conditioned to view things differently.

It does little good to say that the sexes ought not to be conditioned differently. The fact of the matter is—we are! And we can thank God for this. As Ben Franklin said, "It is the man and woman united that make the complete human being." The differences we bring to marriage make the relationship interesting, mutually beneficial, and challenging. These differences complement and "complete" us. The differences make for conflict, but the resulting growth is worth it all.

Communication with God

One aspect of communication that secular books neglect, that enhances good communication between husband and wife, is communication with God.

From a Christian perspective, our relationship with God must come first. As Jesus said, we are only to worship God, not our husband, wife, children, parents, in-laws, or things. Many marriages falter and fail because we fail to maintain open, honest communication with God. The teachings of both Moses and Jesus place our relationship with God *before* our social relationships. When we are properly related to God, our interaction with our spouse and children is more constructive and profitable (Deuteronomy 6:4-5; Leviticus 19:18; Mark 12:28-31).

Every pastor can tell of parishioners who were having serious marital problems, but when *both* husband and wife got into a right relationship with God—they both became reconciled to each other. When *both* partners yield their lives to God, then both are guided by the same principles. Couples who put God first, find that once the lines of communication with God are opened, those between husband and wife begin to open up, and relationships begin to improve.

Of course a happy relationship in marriage presumes that *both* share this common commitment. When it is *not* mutual, when one or both renege on their commitment, when one or both fail to keep their lines of communication with God open, maintaining the marriage becomes more difficult. But where there is a mutual desire to strive for oneness through obedience to God and Christ, then growth in marriage is the inevitable result.

When we are faithful to our commitment to God, we stay actively involved in the Christian church and community, and we stay in touch with God through Bible reading, prayer, and meditation. In this way God's principles can provide the direction and guidance we need to live productively. When both partners rest in God, they not only build on a solid foundation, but they are drawn closer to God and to one another.

A word of caution is in order at this point about the insidious way that pride obstructs communication with God and our spouse. Pride leads to self-righteousness and estrangement from God. It tells us, "I'm okay! I'm right! But my spouse is wrong!" Pride keeps us from admitting that we are the ones who are wrong. Pride keeps us from saying "I'm sorry," and from asking for forgiveness. Pride keeps us from turning the other cheek. Pride creates a wall between husband and wife, between parent and child. Daily contact with God helps us stay in touch with sound principles for harmonious family relationships.

Reasons We Do Not Communicate Well

Before considering effective ways of communicating with our spouse, let us mention at least three reasons why we don't.

1. *Fear* is probably the primary reason we don't communicate well. We're afraid of getting hurt. We're afraid our spouse may laugh, yell, condemn, or reject what we have to say. (For example: "That's a stupid idea. Where did you ever get that?" "Of all the idiotic ideas you've come up with, that takes the cake!" "What do you think? Money doesn't grow on trees!") When we are put down a time or two, we soon learn that if we don't want to get hurt, it's best to keep quiet. Fear may also be a problem if we had been put down so much as a child that we dare not risk humiliation from our spouse.

Often a married person will say, "My husband (or wife)

doesn't want to talk to me." But when we examine their communication pattern closely, we find the reason behind their failure to communicate is the *way* one responds to the other. Harsh responses can lead to a breakdown in communication because the one spouse is continually attacked and rejected.

Joseph and Lois Bird use the analogy of "flight distance" among animals to illustrate why some couples do not communicate very well. Wild animals have their own territory. When other animals approach, they either defend their territory or flee. Domesticated animals, however, will allow people to walk right up to them. In marriage we can work at reducing the "distance" and creating an environment conducive to closeness. Our spouse needs to feel free to talk and to share. One way we can do this is by not being judgmental, sarcastic, or censorious—practices that are all unconducive to openness in communication.

2. Another reason we may not communicate well is that *we may not have been trained well at home*. If we come from a home in which good, constructive communication was the practice, fine. But if it was *not* the pattern, then unknowingly we will have picked up negative communication patterns. Even though we have vowed not to incorporate our parents' destructive practices into our marriage, when we are under pressure the old ways rise to the surface and, before we know it, we are expressing ourselves just as Mom and Dad did. Fortunately, patterns can be changed, but it requires the will to change, hard work, and time.

It is helpful to remember that our wife is *not* our mother, nor is our husband our father! This is especially true if we have come into a marriage with a lot of "negative baggage." We need to practice the positive qualities that we wish to live by, those we have developed, as well as those we have learned from others.

3. A third reason we may not communicate well is that *we may be plagued with a feeling of insecurity*. Often insecurity is compensated for by being aggressive, domineering, and/or authoritative. We may strike out at our spouse, criticizing, and belittling our partner in an attempt to build up our own ego. It is dif-

ficult for a spouse to communicate and cope with an overbearing, loud person. We need to realize that we cannot build up our ego by tearing down someone else's. Scripture says that we "find ourselves" by serving, helping, and building up others. God does not ask us to condemn others, but to build one another up in love.

Hindrances to Good Communication

Now let's turn our attention to a consideration of some of the significant obstacles to good communication.

1. A first hindrance is the desire to only talk about *safe areas.* Sometimes our past experiences at communicating didn't go too well. Perhaps our parents did not respect our input, or they may have ignored and ridiculed our suggestions. In such cases we have been conditioned not to speak freely, or at least not until we felt it was safe. But in a warm, loving, supportive marital setting, past negative backgrounds *can* be overcome. If we know that we will be "pounced on with both feet," or that we will meet with rejection, we will naturally avoid those vulnerable areas. We may also be afraid of angering our partner and suffering the consequences of this anger.

Unfortunately, the subjects we avoid are the very ones we should discuss for stability and growth in the marriage: husband/wife roles, money, children, in-laws, sex, religion, and work.

2. A second hindrance to good communication is created when we *erect barriers.* We may put up a protective shield between ourselves and our spouse in the form of a television show, newspaper, magazine, or book. We are not saying that a couple should not watch TV., but watching it does cut down on opportunities to share with one's spouse and children, particularly during mealtimes. The evening meal can be a good opportunity for sharing together the events of the day. It may be the only time in the day when the entire family is together. It is wise to use this time in the most productive and positive manner for the whole family.

There are other types of barriers that we can erect. For example, children may retreat to their rooms and turn up their stereo to make communication difficult. Working extra hours limits the time for communication. Even the way one sits in the home can limit discussion. Sitting with one's back to another person is not likely to encourage conversation. It is helpful to become aware of the subtle ways we erect barriers and to evaluate our total communication pattern. If there are ways that we hide from each other, we need to ask, "Why are we hiding?" "What are our problems?" "Why don't we open up and share?"

3. A third obstacle to effective communication is when a spouse *takes an authoritative position* on issues. It's difficult to live with someone who wants to have the final word on everything. If one spouse always thinks he or she is right, why should the other bother to talk? "Just tell me, O Master or Mistress!" If a spouse always insists on being right, the other will often become passive or agree to preserve the peace.

But there is a limit to everything. Eventually the quiet one will explode. The explosion is usually a verbal outburst, although at times it may involve some drastic action. When we read or hear of a couple whom we thought were "so compatible," who are now "suddenly" getting a divorce, there is a good chance that there were serious communication problems that went unattended. Usually these cases are the end result of extensive conflict and passivity. The escapee says in desperation, "I just can't take it anymore. I have to get out!"

Also, dominated spouses have a way of getting back at their oppressors. Sometimes a "headache" is the wife's way of saying, "You can't treat me like that and get away with it." Or the workaholic husband may be escaping from what he views as a hopeless situation. "At least at work I'm appreciated," he thinks. Or "At least at work, I'm my own boss!"

Where do we learn these domineering techniques? Many of them are ones we have carried into marriage from experiences at home, from our family of origin, and from experiences growing out of it.

4. A critical fourth hindrance that blocks effective communi-

cation is *not listening* to what our spouse is saying. While this is usually associated with some of the other hindrances, it is a serious problem in its own right. Sometimes people don't listen to their spouse because they feel that they are superior. Why listen when what the other person has to say isn't important anyway?

Sometimes wives or husbands don't listen because they have learned from past experience that their response would only be ignored, rejected, or ridiculed. So why speak? Sometimes we don't listen because we feel that we know what is right and we don't have time to waste listening. We may feel that it's more important to use the time we would spend listening to phrase our response to our "inferior" spouse. Or we may not listen because we are preoccupied with other thoughts, whether they revolve around children, work, the home, or other persons.

5. A fifth hindrance to good communication is using "you" statements, *analyzing,* and *labeling* our spouse. If we say, "You always forget to have my shirts ready," or, "You never remember my birthday," our spouse is bound to be antagonized. Also, using derogatory terms, such as, "You're frigid," "You're neurotic," "You're a sloppy housekeeper," "You're an insensitive husband," will alienate our mate! Paul's advice in Philippians 4:6-8 and in 1 Corinthians 13:4-8a are certainly relevant here. If we hope to improve communication, frontal attacks and ruthless name-calling are not the way to go about it.

A version of this hindrance is placing blame. When blame is placed, one spouse determines that no matter what has happened, it is not that person's fault. Either someone else or something else has caused it. Many times an innocent spouse is blamed for the poor communication in the marriage. In these situations we may hear one spouse say, "It's your fault we never talk; you're insensitive and don't listen," without acknowledging the fact that the time for talking may not have been appropriate. For example, a wife may choose to talk just before bedtime when her husband is tired and sleepy. It's important for each partner to take responsibility for their own actions and behaviors when it comes to communication. None of us is perfect in the way we communicate with our spouse. We must take responsibility for what we say and not blame the other person for all the problems.

6. A sixth hindrance to good communication is *sending double messages*. The wife sending a double message may respond to her husband's request for affection with words like, "Yes, we can have sex if you want to, but my stomach is really upset and I feel like I'm going to be sick!" The husband who says to his wife, "Sure, we could buy that automatic dishwasher, but we will have to stop the kids' music lessons for a couple of years," is also sending confusing, conflicting messages. Sending a double message is not only frustrating, but it antagonizes a spouse and shuts down communication.

Double messages come in both verbal and nonverbal form. The husband may agree verbally to share grocery shopping responsibilities, but continually put off doing it. A wife might say that she really wants to visit his relatives, but at the agreed upon time is not ready to go. The wife may say yes to her husband's desire for sex, but put on a flannel nightgown, curl up in a ball in bed, and turn her back to him. These double messages can both confuse and anger our spouse. If we hope to improve communication, we must level with our spouse and send clear messages.

7. Additional hindrances might be called *individual patterns of communication*. All husbands and wives develop their own unique communication patterns. While many of these are good and positive, some are not. For example, *lack of selectivity in talking* to our spouse is one such pattern. Some people boast, "I say just what's on my mind." Most counselors agree that we should not "let it all hang out." Some things are best left unsaid. Furthermore, we may not have all the facts. Sometimes by waiting, or by some low-key questioning and listening we find that our judgment or evaluation of the situation or event was incorrect. It's always best to weigh our words carefully—erring on the side of silence.

Another problem is the *"babbling brook,"* or constant talker.

It's difficult to talk with someone who "never comes up for air." If we have a pattern of monopolizing the conversation, small wonder our spouse does not want to talk. How could the other person get a word in edgewise?

Still another hindrance is a pattern of *constantly arguing*. A spouse who is insecure may try to demonstrate superiority or "intelligence" by arguing over every bit of trivia. This not only drives the other partner up the wall, but the partner learns that it is pointless to respond, since additional input is not really valued anyway. Or it may only result in another argument.

Finally, good communication is blocked by those who *continually interrupt* their spouse. Often we find spouses who never let their mates finish a statement, story, or joke. Such spouses constantly interrupt because they feel that what they have to say is so much more important than what their spouse might say. They think they know it all; they are rude. They show no respect for their spouse.

Scripture clearly teaches that we should not think more highly of ourselves than we ought to think (Romans 12:3). We are finite creatures. We need all the help we can get. A loving spouse welcomes the input of the partner showing the respect and courtesy the other person deserves.

Other hindrances to good communication could be added to those above. The important point is this: if we allow our ego, pride, and insecurity to stand in the way of eliminating the barriers that separate us from the ones we love, and to hinder growth in our relationships, neither partner gains.

Rules for Good Communication

Do not despair. The communication tools and skills that follow can help improve the interaction in any marriage. They may require some time to master, but they are worth the effort. The negative habits we developed during our formative years have become "second nature." We express them spontaneously, without thinking. Now in our marriage we face the task of eliminating them, while we enlarge our good communication skills. As we are doing this, we have the task of also blending *two* diverse subcultures (yours and your spouse's) into a new *one*. We can succeed in doing this in marriage if both husband and wife commit themselves to the task.

The following are general rules that all can implement if we truly want better communication in our marriage.

1. The first rule involves *timing, location,* and *atmosphere. Timing* is incredibly important if we want good communication to take place. We simply cannot discuss problems and concerns with our spouse at just anytime of the day or night and expect positive results. For example, attempting to begin a conversation about something of major concern in the morning as one spouse is rushing off to work is not appropriate. Morning is usually a time of rising anxiety, and of diverted attention. Although just before bedtime may be good for some couples, it could present difficulty if one or both spouses is too tired to think clearly. Immediately upon arriving home from work can prove to be difficult. After dinner, when the children are doing homework or when they are in bed for the evening may be a good choice.

Location is also an important consideration. If the children do their homework in the kitchen, then it is not an appropriate place to talk, for both parents and children will be disturbed. A walk may give a couple some private time, or going into a room and closing the door.

And the *atmosphere* must be conducive to discussion. If tension is high in the home, for whatever reason, it's better to wait until both partners are relaxed and somewhat settled.

2. *Self-awareness* is a second rule of good communication. This involves being aware of our own thoughts, feelings, and wants. Although this may appear to come naturally and require little effort, this is rarely the case. Dr. Williams cites a situation in which a lack of self-awareness proved detrimental. After a trying day, the wife was unaware that she was looking for some support and understanding. She proceeded to slam cupboard doors, bang

pans about, and generally mumble and grumble. Anger and disappointment began to rise, as her husband retreated to the farthest corner of the house. She was unaware, not only of her desire for understanding, but also of her behavior. If she had taken the time to think about her wants and her feelings, she could have altered her behavior and allowed her husband to get close and give her the support she desired. If communication is not going well, we need to ask ourselves, "How am I behaving and speaking?" "What is it that I want or need?" and "What are my true thoughts and feelings?"

3. *Sending a clear message* is the third rule of good communication. We should state clearly what we have in mind. No hidden agendas. No deception. No double messages. It is important to provide accurate and honest information. Some counselors call this leveling. Leveling means being transparent, authentic, and explicit about how we feel.

A major component of a clear message is self-disclosure. This involves an open and honest sharing of personal thoughts and feelings. Self-disclosure helps a partner to understand the other to the fullest extent. This allows the spouse to feel understood and close to the other, assuming the other is warm and accepting. It stimulates feelings of trust and deepens the relationship. Communication will never be effective and meaningful unless both partners are willing to level with each other.

A tape that was shared with a class on marriage (recorded by Dr. G. Timothy Leville, director of Family Life Education for the Family Service of Philadelphia) points up the importance of sending a clear message. After a lengthy evening seminar on the family, Dr. Leville returned home at about midnight. Soon after he arrived, his wife said to him, "Boy, it sure would be nice to have some donuts, wouldn't it?" As he got up to go, she said, "No, don't go, you've been out late and you're tired." So he settled down beside her on the sofa to watch a little TV and unwind. After a while she said, "Boy, it *sure* would be nice to have those donuts!" Although this angered him, he went out and bought the donuts. And he added, "They were good donuts!"

When the donut incident was shared with a group of young people, one woman said, "If I were he, I would have told her to go out and buy them herself! She wasn't a cripple!" Obviously, the woman's response reveals an insensitive, hostile attitude. While it's true that Mrs. Leville should have given a clear message, Mr. Leville—who knew his wife well—did the loving thing. As a result, both profited. While people differ in their opinion as to who was to blame for the misunderstanding in the donut incident, sending a clear message could have avoided much of the confusion.

4. A fourth crucial factor in good communication is *listening*. When our spouse is talking, we must focus and concentrate on the message, not on our own thoughts or what we are going to say next. It can be helpful to both spouses if the receiver of the message *reflects* it back to the sender. For example, Mary might say, "I like visiting your parents, but it sure causes me to feel stress and tension." Her husband, Jim, might reflect the message back to her by saying, "It's not always easy for you to visit my parents, but there are parts of the visit that you enjoy and you wouldn't mind seeing them again." Mary can then respond, "Yes, that's what I'm saying," or "No, that's not what I'm saying." This allows Jim to determine whether he was accurate in his interpretation, and Mary can feel that she is understood. Of course, such reflection is not done in every conversation, but when the topics are important, reflecting can be helpful.

An additional component in listening is *empathy*. Empathy is putting yourself in the other person's place, to feel how your spouse feels, to understand intimately your spouse's thoughts and feelings. This intense understanding reinforces and aids in the development of trust, honesty, and respect in the marriage.

In the absence of empathy and reflective listening, some husbands and wives resort to *mind reading*. We assume that we know what our spouse is thinking or feeling. This is the source of many marital conflicts. Since we cannot know our spouse's thoughts or motives, it makes sense to ask exactly what was meant, or if what we *think* is true is *actually* true. It's suprising how many times we are wrong in our assessment. Many problems can be avoided if we don't assume we know what the other is thinking, and ask what is really meant.

5. The fifth rule for good communication is to discuss problems and concerns when both are *feeling good* or are in a good mood. Intense feelings such as anger or hurt are not usually a good context for communication. It's best to let these feelings subside before we try to discuss an important matter. Many times when we are at the height of our anger, we are under emotional strain and we often say things that we later regret. Taking time to calm down makes a rational conversation possible. We are less likely to regret what we say if we wait until the heat of the moment has passed.

6. A sixth rule is *talk about communication*. For example, during the engagement period of one couple, there were times when disagreements arose while on the telephone. The woman had a tendency to hang up on her fiance, leaving him confused. During a calm moment when they were together, he said, "I have a hard time when you hang up on me. It makes me feel hurt and angry. It really solves nothing. Can we agree that from now on if we have a disagreement you won't hang up on me?" They talked about how they communicated and set up some ground rules.

Although this may seem like a tedious task, it can make a positive difference in our communication. It helps tremendously when we take the time to identify problem areas of communication and, during a *calm* moment, sit down with our spouse and set up some rules for communicating.

The above rules can help persons achieve positive communication in marriage. But they will not improve our marriage until we put them into practice. While this takes effort, the end result will be a more harmonious relationship and greater happiness for all concerned. Following the rules of good communication is one more way we can put love to work in marriage.

CHAPTER 6

CONFLICT AND ANGER IN MARRIAGE
Resolution and Management

No one can live with anyone for any length of time or in any meaningful way without conflict. It's virtually impossible to do.[1] The only people who don't have difficulty are those who live on a superficial level, and those who have only known each other for a short time. Even our Lord had difficulty communicating with his intimate disciples. Who are we to think that we could breeze through life free of conflict and free of anger?

No matter how hard we try to live harmoniously with our spouse, conflict and anger will arise. So if we experience conflict and anger, *we're normal!* If we don't, we are probably lying, or living on a superficial level, or both!

Root Causes of Conflict

There are many reasons why conflict arises. One of the root causes is simply our *finitude*. We don't know everything, and even that which we know is only fragmentary. We will inevitably make mistakes in our judgments, statements, and actions. We bring limited knowledge, as well as limited understanding and experience, to each issue.

When we approach any topic or problem, each of us will probably see it somewhat differently. This is not necessarily "bad," nor need it be a cause for an argument. Instead, it can be an occasion for us pool our knowledge and our insight, and to work for better understanding and a solution of the issue at hand. This sounds good, but approaching differences this way does not come naturally, because we have a tendency to want to have our own way and be right!

Another root cause of conflict between marriage partners is *pride*. If we can set pride aside, then we can approach conflict as an opportunity to resolve a problem or issue constructively. Humility provides a broader base of understanding on which to build our marriage.

A third root cause of conflict is a *poor self-image*. Because our concept of "self-worth" may be low, we may strike out at others, feeling that aggression will compensate and cover up our insecurity. Often such individuals are chronic fault-finders—critics of everything. Nothing is right with the world—people, the economy, schools, government, and the church. Everything is seen as going from bad to worse.

A fourth root cause of conflict in marriage is *lack of agreement about roles* (expected behavior of husband/father and wife/mother), and family goals. Basic conflict is often latent, something of which we are not consciously aware. If a husband's mother waited on his dad, he assumes that his wife will do the same when they marry. If a wife's father was helpful around the house and shared in doing household chores, she assumes that her husband will also help out in the home. Husbands and wives should realistically face differences in role definitions, and try to reach consensus on what their roles should be. They should also seriously discuss marital and family goals. Unless they do, serious conflict will persist.

Conflict also arises regarding the use of time and money, and over children, in-laws, religion, work, and on and on the list goes. Some of this is inevitable, since we continue to change and grow as individuals. For example, the personal changes that occur as we move into parenthood are many. With the addition of every child the potential for conflict increases.

Barriers to Conflict Resolution

Just as there are barriers to good communication, so there are barriers to conflict resolution. Obviously, the barriers to good communication and those to conflict resolution will overlap, because we communicate when we resolve conflict. Following are some barriers that, if removed, will help us both to resolve conflict and to maintain good communication.

1. A major barrier to conflict resolution is *the refusal to acknowledge that the problem exists.* Although both spouses may know what the problem is, they may refuse to bring it out into the open. It may be a very sensitive problem, emotionally charged for one or both of them. Or one spouse may hesitate to talk about the problem because of fear of the response of the other. Again one partner may have been taught not to talk about particular topics, such as sex. Even though much conflict arises over sex in marriage, for many it is a taboo subject. Whatever the reason may be for failing to face the conflict-causing areas, it is obvious that there can be no resolution of the problem until both recognize it and are willing to face it squarely.

2. Related to the refusal to acknowledge the problem is *focusing on the symptoms rather than the causes of the conflict.* For example, the wife may be concerned about her husband's unwillingness to assume responsibility for things around the house. Originally they had agreed to share household tasks. Instead of dealing with this issue, the wife "nags" her husband for not picking up his socks. In reality, not picking up the socks is only a small part of the real problem of assuming responsibility for one's own personal effects and for the division of labor in the home.

3. Attacking our wife or husband—that is, *blaming and name-calling*—is another barrier to conflict resolution. Although in many homes the attack is kept on a verbal level, in other homes, physical abuse occurs. From a Christian perspective this is totally unacceptable. Those who engage in physical *and* psychological abuse should seek out a good counselor or therapist.

In some cases a period of separation is helpful, not only for the abused spouse but also for the abuser.

4. Another barrier to conflict resolution and good communication is *when one spouse refuses to accept any responsibility for the conflict.* This person resorts to blaming the partner for the entire situation. "You" messages are continually used, such as— "you did this," or "You did that," or "It's all *your* fault." As noted before, none of us is perfect. Each must assume responsibility for his or her share of the problem. This means admitting our shortcomings or mistakes. Not only do we need to admit our part in the problem, but also assume responsibility for solving it. When an individual takes responsibility the statements change from "You" messages to "I" messages. For example, "*I* have been attacking you," and "*I* will work at eliminating that behavior."

5. *Extreme anger* also acts as a barrier to conflict resolution. Anger can influence us to do and say things that we would not choose to do or say in calmer moments. Much of the time, conflict involves anger. If anger rises to high levels, it is best to let it subside and deal with the problem at a later time.

6. A final barrier is *fatigue.* A conflict will likely remain unresolved if either partner is tired. Thoughts can become confused and tempers are generally shorter when we are fatigued. Resolving the problem may take longer; or we may agree with our spouse quickly in order to find some peace, without having arrived at a satisfactory resolution. It is best to wait until both spouses are rested before tackling major conflict.

If we can avoid these barriers, we can move ahead to resolve conflict constructively. In the process we will achieve greater rapport with our spouse. Each resolution brings with it greater understanding and appreciation of each other.

Steps to Conflict Resolution

The steps to effective conflict or problem resolution are similar to those needed for effective communication.

First, identify the problem. This sounds easier than it sometimes is. Many times we argue around the problem, and we have conflict over a situation which actually is an outgrowth of the original problem. Sometimes when we have conflict over an issue that we cannot identify, we argue over irrelevant things because of the rising hostility related to the real problem. The example of the husband's breach of a previous agreement to do housework and his failure to pick up his socks illustrates this point. The wife focused on the symptom—a room littered with socks—rather than the real cause of the problem, his refusal to share in household chores. Obviously, dealing with the symptom will never cure the problem.

Second, identify all possible solutions. Brainstorm the issue/problem. List *all* of the possible solutions, no matter how worthless one may think they are. Just jot them down.

Third, rank the suggested solutions according to their suitability and worth, discarding all but the best two or three ideas. Critically evaluate these, listing the pros and cons of each.

Fourth, select the best solution.

Fifth, accept it and implement it.

Sixth, after a specified period of time, review its suitability, and make any necessary changes. If you cannot change things, learn from this experience for future problem-solving ventures.

Remember, assuming that you are a reasonable person who is married to another reasonable person, most problems can be resolved. Obviously, both will not always agree enthusiastically and wholeheartedly on the solution or proposed action. But compromising and supporting one another is part of putting love to work.

Conflict Resolution vs. Conflict Management

Since all conflict cannot be resolved, we must accommodate to one another, and also learn to manage conflict. George Hillery, Jr.,[2] points out that conflicts are best *resolved* through facing issues and differences squarely, taking into account feedback that each spouse provides and, as amiably as possible, compromising to reach a mutually satisfactory solution.

But conflict *management*, Hillery notes, means that we deal with the emotional frustration and stress that results from *not* being able to resolve the issue or problem. In such cases we must learn to live with the problem. We must accept the fact that there are legitimate differences in beliefs and practices that each may not wish to give up. Mature people do this all the time, so long as there is no breach of ethics or morality. In such cases, people agree to disagree (see 1 Corinthians 8).

People have devised various acceptable ways of managing conflict when they reach an impasse. Some go for long walks, walking until they feel things are under control, and then returning to live with the difference. Others find help through prayer and meditation. Still others engage in sports or vigorous exercise to get rid of tension, stress, and hostility that may have been generated by the impasse.

But the bottom line is realizing that none of us can have our own way all the time! We *are* different from one another, and these differences will sometimes result in conflicts that cannot be resolved. Just as a wife puts up with things that she does not like about her husband, so a husband must learn to adapt and accept habits and decisions that are not necessarily to his liking. These issues are usually not moral ones, but merely matters of personal preference.

In summary, good communication and conflict resolution begins when we accept the fact that all couples have problems in these areas. Change only comes about when we begin to work at those skills and techniques that are needed to develop a sense of oneness. Both spouses benefit when each is willing to give more than to take. Unconditional commitment and unconditional love provide a strong foundation on which to build. Agreeing on role definitions and family goals also contributes to the development of harmonious interaction within marriage.

But no matter how hard we try, disagreements, disappointments, conflicts, problems, and anger are things we *cannot* escape. But with God's help, mature love, and honest effort conflicts can be resolved, compromised, or managed so that we can grow in marital harmony and happiness.

Anger Can Be Controlled

Anger, however, is bound to be generated while discussing and arguing through an issue. Tempers will fly. How high they fly depends on our temperament, the stress we are under at the time, and the intensity we may feel about the issue. The problem resolution skills we have brought into our marriage are also a key factor. It is important to realize that everyone gets angry. And there is nothing wrong with anger, so long as we keep it under control. Most wrongs in society have been righted by people who became angry about an issue and did something about it. Gains have been made in labor conditions, wage disputes, civil rights, women's rights, drunk driving, and the like when people become angry enough to organize and work to solve the problem.

So anger is not necessarily an evil. What we want to avoid, however, is bottling it up and allowing it to explode. The apostle Paul urges us, "Do not let the sun go down while you are still angry" (Ephesians 4:26). It is usually when we fail to diffuse our anger that an explosion occurs. When this does happen we find the explosion comes over some trifling thing--trifling especially when compared with the large things that have been "swept under the rug." The apostle James reminds us that our lack of control of anger "does not bring about the righteous life that God desires" (James 1:20). And the writer of Proverbs (15:18) tells us that a hot-tempered person stirs up dissension, but a person who is patient calms a quarrel. All we learn from giving vent to our anger in unacceptable ways is how to do so with greater force and volume. Anger is fine, so long as it is controlled and channeled in a constructive manner.

Work at Conflict Resolution When Not Angry

While Paul's advice, "Do not let the sun go down while you

are still angry," is sound, it is often misinterpreted. He is not suggesting that it is possible to be free of anger, nor that we can or should always "kiss and make up" immediately. Some problems take time to think through and resolve. One often finds that time spent in prayer and thoughtful meditation helps.

What Paul does counsel, however, is that we should not retain our anger and stew about it. That will not help. Cool the anger, and agree to work on the problem at some future date when both are in a proper frame of mind. Do whatever is necessary to get things under control. Sometimes it is good to let time elapse, and then tackle the problem when both have their wits about them. If we find that we cannot resolve the problem, then it is best to seek the help of a competent counselor.

In resolving conflict we must guard against selfish pride that keeps us from *leveling,* from being honest and open in our talk and communication. If we are seeking the "right" or correct solution, then we will welcome help and truth no matter where it comes from--especially from our spouse! On every issue under consideration there is "his" point of view or "her" point of view, and *all the other* points of view neither is considering. Our goal in good communication, in conflict resolution, or in problem solving is always the same. The goal is to do the "right" thing, to do the functional or constructive thing that will build the marriage up in love. Who is right is of little consequence. What we are seeking is the will of God for us. And it is God's will that we work to become one, build each other up in love, and find fullness of life by glorifying God.

CHAPTER 7

SEX IN MARRIAGE
An Act of Love

Several years ago one of the authors spoke in a church to a couples' club composed mostly of married people. The topic for the evening was, "Sex, Love, and Marriage." After the meeting a well-dressed middle-aged woman said to her husband who came into the meeting after the talk was finished, "Oh John, you should have been here. He just gave the most wonderful talk about sex and marriage!" To which he wryly replied, "What did he talk about? How to be happy *without it*?" One could not help but think from the verbal exchange between them, and the tension in the air, that this couple was not particularly well adjusted in their sex life.

Despite all the talk about sex that goes on today, genuine communication about sexuality is all too rare between married people. Unfortunately we bring too many distorted notions into our marriages--information we picked up as adolescents from our peers, from the mass media, and even from church. The media too often emphasizes the physical aspects of sex in an unrestrained, sensuous manner, while ministers tend to dwell on the immorality of contemporary society without giving much positive guidance.

True, both the Old and New Testaments frequently mention sex in and outside of marriage as a perennial problem for humans. But there are also many positive references to sexuality in the Scriptures. For example, the Old Testament book, The Song of Solomon, is entirely devoted to the beauty and wonder of physical love. Many other references throughout the Bible affirm the integral nature of sex and love in marriage.

Sexual Intimacy Is Vital

Sexual intimacy is a vital, necessary, enjoyable part of a good marriage. Sex is also *one* of the ways we express our love for our spouse, a way both partners receive pleasure and physiological release, and the way we procreate the race. And we list these in order of their importance. If you feel uncomfortable with what we have written thus far, we believe you have a problem with the concept of sexuality and with sex in marriage.

If a husband said to his wife, "Honey, let's park the kids with one of our parents or with a sitter and let's get away for a weekend--just the two of us!" And if her response was, "There he goes again; he just wants to get me away so he can have a sex orgy," then we would say that she has an attitudinal problem, a serious communication problem, or a problem in her sexual adjustment. If the wife received an equally negative response from her husband, he has a problem that needs attention. If either of the spouses find themselves dreading or fearing intimacy, then we strongly recommend counseling.

The Sex and Hunger Drives

From a Christian perspective, not to mention a human perspective, sex is good. It belongs in marriage. It is a God-given drive that seeks satisfaction, just as our desire for food motivates us to seek satisfaction from our physical hunger. Both our appetite for food and our desire for affection are renewed each day, and it is normal to feel the need for both.

While we don't necessarily need to have sexual intercourse every day, we do need to feel loved and wanted. We want our spouse to express this love with appropriate behavior. We want to know that our partner cares. We not only like to be stroked or touched, but we appreciate hearing love verbalized.

Affectional Needs Persist

Most people rightly associate sex with love, and certainly as Christians we believe they go together. We also believe that love needs to be demonstrated in tangible ways. We are physical, as well as spiritual beings, with desires and drives that seek expression and satisfaction.

In an earlier chapter we wrote about communication. Obviously if we are not communicating well as husband and wife this will affect our desire to give and receive physical expressions of love. But even if we are not communicating perfectly, our desire for physical intimacy still persists. This is why Scripture reminds us that we do not belong to ourselves, but to our spouse, and that we have the privilege and obligation to share our bodies with one another through sexual intercourse (1 Corinthians 7:2-5). It also cautions us not to deny our spouse's desire for sexual intimacy for any sustained period of time.

The Bible says that when we marry we are to strive to become one (Mark 10:6-8). This oneness expresses itself not only by sharing common values and goals in the marriage, but also through sexual intimacy.

As we noted earlier, the apostle Paul urges us not to let the sun go down while we are still angry. While we cannot always resolve all problems immediately, we can at least cool our anger, and agree to seek an amicable solution to the problem in the near future. Being the astute observer of marital interaction that he was, Paul observed that too many marriages were disrupted by poor communication that often led to physical infidelity. Therefore, he counseled that husbands and wives should try to live in a reconciled state. In this way they would not be tempted to look elsewhere for satisfaction of their affectional needs.

Some might argue that a spouse should be able to control physical desires, saying, "After all we're not animals. We are civilized." Our response is that most individuals do control their sexual desires and do act as humans. Nonetheless, the sex drive is very strong, and all too often marital relations are disrupted by physical infidelity. This does not occur just because a spouse is "oversexed!" In most cases, the root cause of unfaithfulness stems from a breakdown in communication, a feeling of alienation, of being neglected or rejected on the part of one or both partners. The need for physical intimacy, for love and understanding, cannot be denied or willed away. If we hope to have happy marriages, we must accept the fact that we are sexual beings, and that our needs, and some of our wants, must be satisfied.

Many readers may say, "We have not experienced physical infidelity in our marriage, but our sexual relationship leaves something to be desired." As Christians, we still may be tempted to have a sexual affair, but our values and beliefs help to keep our behavior in check. But conflict and poor communication can create a barrier to a rewarding sexual relationship. Sex simply ceases. Husbands become frustrated, impatient, and angry while wives become confused, disappointed, and indifferent.

With physical infidelity eliminated as an option, this situation can become a vicious cycle. A breakdown in communication can lead to strained sexual relationships which can lead to further communication problems and conflicts. The cycle can last throughout a marriage. When sexual intimacy does occur, which is usually on an infrequent basis, it is strained and less than pleasurable and satisfying. Sexual dysfunctions, such as impotence for men, painful intercourse for women, or loss of desire for either may develop. This can lead to further problems both in sexual performance and in communication.

Sex Will Not Solve Communication Problems

A word of caution is in order here. Often a husband or wife will try to compensate for feelings of alienation that stem from poor communication by having sex, thinking that the physical act will "bring them closer." Unfortunately, all it does is bring them closer physically. It does not remove the wall they have erected between themselves.

For a couple who are not "one" in a spiritual or

psychological sense, physical sex may provide physiological release, but it will not resolve their communication problems. Poor communication needs to be remedied. For it is only after this takes place that sexual intimacy will make two one and will provide the enjoyable experience God intended it to be.

If a spouse refuses to have sex with the mate because they are "having problems," this will only compound the problem. The denied spouse will probably interpret the refusal to be intimate as another evidence of rejection and a lack of love. The best way to correct the marital discord is to continue to be intimate while the problems are being worked out. This is one way to show that we still love our spouse and are willing to meet affectional needs.

Sex Drives and Desires Vary

We are indebted to the sexual liberation movement, as well as to the women's liberation movement for pointing out that many so-called physiological differences related to the sex drive of women are really culturally conditioned. But, try as we may to equalize the sexes' desire for sexual intercourse, the husband's drive for sex is apparently still more intense than most wives. However, generally speaking, women's desire does not peak until about mid-life. There is considerable evidence to support the idea that the husband's sex drive is more specific and intense than the wife's. Tensions and problems about the frequency of having sex are common in many marriages.

One researcher asked husbands and wives, "How often do you have sexual intercourse with your husband or wife?" The responses were contradictory. Wives reported having sexual intercourse *more than* their husbands did! What accounted for this discrepancy? Apparently wives reported the number of times their husbands *approached* them about having sex, whereas husbands reported the number of times they *actually* succeeded in having sexual intercourse. Or perhaps the women believed that sex actually occurred too often, whereas men thought it occurred less often than desired.

Why Do Men and Women Differ?

How do we account for the differences between men and women in their desire for various kinds of affection and the frequency of sexual intercourse? Obviously both genetic/biological/hormonal factors and cultural/social/environmental factors play a part. In addition, ethnic/subcultural/socioeconomic class and education level influence one's responses. On a personal level these come into play in the family subculture in which each of us is nurtured. How we react to these experiences contributes both to our attitude toward sexuality and our understanding of it. The specific experiences we encounter during adolescence and adulthood certainly help shape our attitudes and values.

Most people are reared in families in which sex is regarded as something good and enjoyable. Most of us also received some kind of sex instruction from our parents and siblings, as well as from school and peers. Our parents likely instructed us about the wisdom of exercising self-control before marriage. They also assured us that sex before marriage was not "the unpardonable sin." What we are saying is that most readers probably came into marriage with a wholesome outlook on sexuality and with "great expectations." Nonetheless, we probably still suffered from some misinformation.

But some of us may have come into marriage with more than just misinformation. Some probably were handicapped by a variety of hang-ups that we found difficult to overcome. Let us mention just a few:

Some may have had a "bad" experience with members of the opposite sex. As a result we may feel that we were exploited, used, and abandoned.

Others may have been victims of incest or sexual molestation by a parent, relative, or stranger.

Still others may have been given misinformation about the opposite sex by our mother or father, who themselves did not have a healthy outlook on sexuality. For example, a mother may have told her daughter, "Men are beasts; they are only after one thing!" Or "I almost died when I gave birth to you!" Or the father who is an alcoholic and is abusive offered a less than adequate model for his son. To discourage premarital sexual intercourse, some parents may have conveyed the idea that sex is dirty, bad, and undesirable. As a result sexual relationships may be looked at with fear and anxiety.

Such unfortunate experiences condition us unfavorably toward sex within marriage. If this has been our experience, we have three alternatives: (1) we can get help from a competent counselor; (2) we can talk things out openly and honestly with our spouse; or (3) we can do nothing. Obviously the least desirable is to do nothing. We recommend that the couple work things out. However, if the troubled spouse does not feel free to do so, then the help of a competent counselor should be sought.

What Sex Is Not For

We have already noted that sex is for love, pleasure, and for procreation. Here are several things that sexual intercourse is *not* for:

It is *not* for *self*-indulgence, but it is meant to be a mutually shared experience.

It is *not* purely for physical release, although physiological release is part of the experience.

It is *not* to be viewed as an expression of hostility and aggression, although some wives may think that their husbands use it that way.

It is *not* a means of punishment—that is, a way to make the spouse who desires sex "suffer" by denying release.

It is *not* a way of wringing or extracting concessions from a spouse. "Unless you do this or that, or give me this or that. . . ."

No particular virtue or condemnation should be ascribed to the spouse whose desire for sex is greater or lesser than the other's. As we mentioned earlier, appetites for sexual intimacy vary not only between the sexes, but also among members of the same sex, and also over time. What is enough for one husband or wife may not be enough or may be too much for another. When frequency of desire varies, each couple must resolve the matter to their mutual satisfaction. It's their own responsibility.

The Problems of Too Much and Too Little

Two complaints that we frequently encounter in counseling are wives who say, (1) "All he ever thinks about is sex!" or (2) "He never comes near me anymore!"

When a wife accuses her husband of never thinking of anything but sex, the scenario usually runs like this. A husband walks into the room where his wife may be working, standing, or sitting. He puts his arms around her and gives her a kiss. They linger, both hugging and kissing. He becomes sexually aroused and suggests she have sex with him. She becomes indignant, accusing him of having ulterior motives for displaying affection, and then blurts out, "Is that all you ever think about?" Actually what we have here is not an oversexed maniac, but a normal male, who when stimulated wants to have sex.

The wife who finds the timing of his offer inconvenient, may say, "Not just now. I've got other things I must do. Let's wait until later when I can give you all my time and attention, okay?" Or she can put him down with the oft-repeated statement, "Is that all you ever think about?" The wisdom of the first response is that the husband does not feel rejected and she elicits his understanding, whereas in the second response the husband feels totally rejected and unloved.

A British newspaper ran the following article which appeared in *Parade Magazine*. "One of the major reasons for marital failure is the wife's sexual rejection of her husband. The British Medical Association, which each year publishes an advice booklet, "Getting Married," reports one frustrated husband's fictional reproach to his reluctant wife:

"During the past year I have attempted to make love to you 365 times. I succeeded 36 times." Among the rejection reasons:

"We will wake the children"—7 times.

"It's too hot"—15 times.

"The windows are open and the neighbors will hear"—3 times.

"I'm not in the mood"—21 times.

Once a month the wife put on a mudpack for armor, twice she broke into giggles, and—the show stopper—105 times she responded with, "Is that all you ever think about?"

"The author of this fictional letter, Dr. Jack Dominian, consultant psychiatrist and adviser to the Catholic Marriage Guidance Council, believes that wives often say no in order to punish or humble their husbands. Sex therefore 'degenerates from its principal role of communicating love.' By making sex a game or by willfully trying to hurt one's husband, without putting love to work, the purpose of sex is totally lost. Sex is a physical way of demonstrating love; withholding it to punish or humble shows a lack of love."

While Dr. Dominian makes a valid point, it is also important that husbands be responsive to the feelings and needs of their wives. Some women feel that their husbands approach them too often, and at inappropriate times. Women do not have the same sexual response as men, nor are they stimulated as often or as easily. Women explain their sexual responses something like this: "Sex requires a great deal of effort; it is physically, emotionally, and psychologically taxing. The amount of effort needed to concentrate and become aroused is quite great. There are times when this effort cannot be made. Therefore, when a husband continually approaches his wife, he is asking for a great deal more effort from her than he will have to give."

This helps explain why women do not experience orgasm as often as men, and why some women "fake" orgasm. Many women feel that it simply takes too much time and effort. Husbands might benefit more in the long run by being less demanding, and more sensitive to the moods, feelings, and energy level of their wives. This is certainly an aspect of sexual relations that deserves further exploration.

Now in the case where the wife complains that her husband never comes near her, she obviously faces a more complex and difficult problem. He needs counseling. Perhaps there is some latent fear or inhibition that needs to be worked out, or some other deep-seated psychological problem rooted in relationships with his parents. These are best remedied through psychotherapy. Or perhaps he has some physical illness or is taking some medication that is inhibiting his desire and potency of which he is not aware. But if both partners are willing to seek medical or psychological assistance, the problems can be either resolved or lessened.

Intimacy as a Ministry

But even when both are able and willing to be intimate, the desire will not always be of the same intensity for the marriage partners. This seems to be a frequent problem. How can it be worked at? The spouse who least desires sex can view participation as a form of "ministry" to the more desiring spouse. Just as we do a host of other things for each other because we love one another, so a spouse can do this as an act of love.

Another alternative for the more desiring spouse is to view the reduction of desire—a little more abstinence—as an expression of love.

While we know that intensity of desire varies, and that both need not have the same appetites, an agreement needs to be reached for a satisfactory sexual adjustment to be achieved. Otherwise, the least desiring spouse will feel "used" and the more desiring one will feel "unloved and rejected." Time needs to be given to open, honest communication about the best possible experience for both partners.

Agreement is best arrived at through negotiation and compromise. The goal is to make each partner as happy as possible in a framework acceptable to both. There is no magical way this can be achieved. It takes time to negotiate differences, especially when desires differ.

The Importance of Mutual Sensitivity

Since husbands commonly desire sex more than wives do, they need to be sensitive to their wives' needs and feelings more than they usually are. Just because men get an erection when they are sexually aroused does not constitute a *need* for sexual intercourse, any more than the fact that when women become aroused it constitutes a need for them. Considerate husbands take into consideration their wife's total well-being.

For example, pregnant women respond to their condition in different ways. Each needs to be treated with special care and attention. Some experience a new sense of freedom about sexual intercourse, since they don't have to worry about pregnancy. Others may be troubled with nausea, or other side effects from pregnancy. While there are no rules, unless specified by a physician, obviously as pregnancy advances, adjustments need to be made. However, so long as both are well and willing, with a shallow penetration and the use of the rear entry position, there is no reason why affection cannot be shared as long as the couple desires.

In addition, when women are nursing, the vaginal lining and the lubricating fluids may be diminished. Vaginal jellies or foams may be employed to avoid undue friction or pain during intercourse.

There are other times when both need to be especially considerate. When either partner is ill, the last thing on the sick spouse's mind is sex. A woman who has a bladder or vaginal infection will not respond favorably to her husband's sexual advances. When either spouse is depressed, upset, or preoccupied with a problem or concern, the best way to show love is by respecting the need for privacy and showing love through empathic support and understanding. When a child is ill, and during times of mourning, a caring spouse will find more appropriate ways to say, "I love you."

Under normal, daily circumstances we need to show sensitivity. Intimate conversations, gentle caressing and holding are highly desired by women. This may lead to sexual intercourse, but for most women it is a wonderful end in itself. The husband should understand that intercourse may not always contribute to the wife's total well-being, even under normal circumstances. A husband whose desire is greater than his wife's can aid his wife in a more rewarding and desirable sexual relationship if he takes the time to be tender and gentle in their conversations.

When children come into the family, a double admonition is in order—for both the husband and wife. First, the wife needs to remember to involve her husband in the care of the infant and in the care of the children. This not only gives him the sense of participation that he needs as a father and husband, but also frees her to do other things and enjoy some free time. Second, the wife needs to remember that her husband is still there, and that his need for affection continues. Some time should be reserved for him, if romance is to be kept in marriage. Special effort needs to be made during the sometimes hectic and trying days of child rearing.

The husband should remember, likewise, that the arrival of an infant and the presence of children places an added stress and burden on relationships between husband and wife. Some people speak of the arrival of a child as creating a mini crisis in the family. This is certainly true of the first child! Therefore, the husband must lovingly make himself available to help his wife with childcare and household duties. He should take necessary precautions to prevent an unwanted pregnancy. The responsibility for contraception ought not to be thrust upon the wife, but mutually shared to the satisfaction of both partners.

It is also important for the husband to keep romance in the marriage. It helps if he continues "to date his wife," and does those things that please her. He can arrange for special events and evenings out. He can send her flowers or bring her small gifts. He can provide her with warmth, support, and encouragement in her roles of wife and mother and also in her general femininity and womanhood.

Morality in the Bedroom

Now let's address the topic of *positions*, *time*, and *place* in sexual intimacy. We tend to agree with the minister who said, "There is no morality in the marital bedroom." Naturally we exclude any action or behavior that either partner finds unacceptable. We usually recommend that couples read several "How-to" books, or sex manuals. By reading several, a balanced view of intimacy in marriage is obtained. But above all, each spouse needs to "read each other" to learn what pleases one's mate. Every couple is unique. Therefore, whatever husbands and wives find mutually enjoyable is what they should freely share.

When should couples have sex? It ought to be a time that is suitable to both husband and wife. Morning, noon, night—or even the middle of the night can be appropriate. Anytime is ideal, if it is what both want. Of course, when children are present, this presents a special concern. It is difficult for the children to understand why the door to their parents' bedroom is closed or locked, and why those strange noises are emanating from their room. Rather than have little children upset by something they don't understand, wait until a suitable time when the children are sleeping or out of the house.

Regarding place, once more it is a couple's decision. Just as long as there is privacy and mutuality—enjoy!

What about oral-genital sex? Marriage partners stimulate one another in various ways. If oral-genital contact is mutually satisfying, they should be free to enjoy each other. They are the ones involved. For most people, one of the goals of sexual intimacy is pleasure through physical stimulation to the point of orgasm. If a couple choose oral-genital contact as an expression of affectional pleasure, fine. There is nothing *un*-Christian about it. However, we should keep in mind the Christian principles of love and respect for each other. If one spouse finds it unpleasant or unacceptable, that partner's preferences should be honored. Take advantage of all the other ways the spouse is willing to express affection, and be thankful for those expressions of love.

Sexual Intimacy as a Barometer

Sexual love often serves as a barometer for measuring the quality of one's marital relationship—excluding those marriages where physical incapacity and ill health precludes physical intimacy. Where a couple share common values, beliefs, and goals, where a couple communicate well, where a couple has put love to work in all aspects of marriage, there sexual adjustment will be the greatest and most enjoyable. Where these are absent, problems will manifest themselves in the area of sexual intimacy.

All good marriages not only have their problematic areas from time to time in the give and take of everyday life; they also have their pleasures and joys. One idea that helps a good marriage grow stronger is periodic "get aways." Park the children! Take a day or weekend off together! Get away and enjoy whatever turns you both on! Life is too short, at best, to deny each other the love and enjoyment God intended both to share.

CHAPTER 8

CHILD REARING IN MARRIAGE
Principles and Practices

Before most of us have children of our own we feel extremely competent about child rearing. We know how others should raise their children, and we are more than willing to give advice—even when parents don't request it. But something happens to us as we rear our children and they eventually go out on their own. We come to realize the difficulty and complexity of the task. We find that somehow we are not as knowledgeable as we thought we were.

There are many excellent secular and Christian books dealing with child development, discipline, and nurture. Readers who are interested in an extensive treatment should consult one of them. We share here some fundamental principles that will make marriage and family life fuller and happier for both parents and children.

Put Your Spouse First

Even after a child comes into the family, our spouse should be first in terms of commitment and loyalty. When we married, we entered into a covenant with our spouse, promising to "love, honor, and cherish" the other person. We didn't promise to put our parents, in-laws, or children first. One counselee, whose wife never went anywhere unless her sister tagged along, said that one day he had had enough and just exploded. He yelled to his wife, "By golly, when we married you pledged yourself to me, *not* to your _____ sister!" One's husband or wife must take priority in affection and loyalty. Only by so doing can two work to become one, which is the basis for security both for one's spouse and children. Children feel secure not merely from the fact that mom or dad spend time with them, and are supportive of their activities and interests, but when they see their parents love and care for each other. Children draw strength from the close bond of love they perceive between their parents.

It's helpful to remember that children are just that—*children*. They are *not* little adults. When God gives us children, they come with innate intelligence and the raw stuff of personality that is ready to be developed, shaped into wholesome Christian characters and personalities. But how are we to go about shaping our children?

Parenting Models

As parents, we usually end up using some parenting model—some set of principles that hang together and constitute our philosophy of parenting. We will share five parenting models. Each of us will find ourselves fitting into one or more of them. These models were originally formulated by E. E. LeMasters and elaborated on by Lamanna and Riedmann.[1] The first three models are ones that we should avoid like the plague. But, sorry to say, all of us have at one time or another exhibited some of their characteristics.

Parent as Martyr

The parent who adopts the martyr role is one who would do anything for her "dear children." We say *her* dear children because mothers seem to be more vulnerable to this model, although fathers also play it well. Usually the time and energy expended on acts performed for the children are all done under the guise of love. Traits of the martyr parent include waiting on children hand

and foot, picking up after them, nagging them to "get up," "not be late," "go to bed," "do your homework," or whatever. Lamanna and Reidmann say that children usually get this type of parent to buy them whatever they want. These children usually manipulate their parents.

Too often the martyr parent allows communication with the marriage partner to deteriorate, and the parent almost loses his or her identity in the children. In such homes neither the parents nor the children feel free, fulfilled, or independent. Also, children do not develop the skills necessary to function in a responsible adult manner, hindering their ability to cope after they leave home.

Parent as Pal

The second option is that of the parent as pal. In this arrangement an atmosphere of laissez faire prevails in which "kids" set their own agendas—standards, goals, and rules. Pal parents give little guidance or supervision—children mostly do as they please.

Those who follow this model are also doomed to failure. Both parents and children end up losers. Children are not adults. They have neither the years of experience, nor the store of knowledge and wisdom their parents have. They need guidance, and God gave them parents to provide it. Children need to know what is expected of them, and what limits society, as well as the family, places on them. Naturally, as they mature the rules and the limits change, and children are increasingly involved in formulating the rules and limits set for their own well-being, as well as that of the family.

Those who insist on playing pal, unfortunately, are more likely to find their children susceptible to the temptations of delinquency, including alcohol and drug abuse. Such children tend not to act responsibly as they move through adolescence into adulthood because they have no guidelines to follow. They flounder, being battered about by their own whims, never really having a firm foundation on which to make decisions and take action.

Parent as Police Officer

A third model open to us is that of the parent as police officer. While both parents play this role, fathers seem to adopt it more often, although mothers make fine drill sergeants also. Unlike the parent as pal, the "officer" comes down hard on children, multiplying rules and strictly enforcing them all. Punishment is usually harsh, swift, and certain. This parent takes the proverb, "Spare the rod and spoil the child" literally. Often the parent was treated harshly by his or her own parent when a child. The officer parent forgets the admonition of the apostle Paul not to irritate your children (by nagging and harsh treatment), or they will become discouraged (Colossians 3:21).

When discipline is too harsh and tyrannical, many children rebel and become delinquent. School, peers, and children's experiences outside of the home all expose them to an element of democracy that they soon realize is not being practiced by their officer parent(s). Children may also not develop the skills necessary to control their own lives because they developed the habit of looking to others to make decisions for them. Sometimes these children, as they leave home, look for substitute parents such as a paramilitary community, a cult, or a highly regulated college. Once out, they may still be unable to handle their own affairs adequately in an independent fashion.

What children need is *not* harsh dominance, but consistent discipline coupled with unconditional love and understanding. It would do us all good to remember the unfair treatment we may have experienced from authority figures and how it made us feel, and then vow not to afflict our children in similar ways.

Parent as Teacher and Counselor

The fourth model, utilizing the developmental perspective of child rearing, views children as flexible and moldable. This parent sees children as people with unlimited potential for growth, and tries to tap their resources to help them develop their full potential in every way.

While this model offers the child the guidance and support needed, it assumes that parents are all-knowing or omniscient. Although children often believe this and count on parental stability, when it comes to decisions and actions, we are not always correct. And we must be willing to admit this when we are wrong.

This model also assumes that parents can be there all the time, whenever the child needs them. Unfortunately, this is not true for several reasons. Not only do most fathers work away from the home, but this is increasingly true for mothers who work outside of the home. Other important commitments, such as obligations to our spouse or the church may also restrict availability to some degree. Giving priority to others and the church at times, helps children to understand the importance of marriage and service to God. Even with the drawbacks of this model, it is one that we personally find attractive. Surely mom and dad together can provide a home environment conducive to growth, as well as the ethical/moral/social instruction and guidance children need.

Parent as Athletic Coach

The fifth parenting model of LeMasters is that of the parent as athletic coach. Again, this model assumes the developmental perspective. As the child ages, parents change the content of their instruction or coaching, granting more and more responsibility to the child. In this model the coach-parent sets the house rules, and enforces them when broken. Children learn to accept discipline and, when necessary, to subordinate their own interests to the needs of the team or family.

But while the coach-parent encourages children to "practice," and watches them grow and develop, the coach-parent realizes that children must play the game of life themselves. Unlike the coach, however, we as parents cannot eject the player from the game, nor can we quit as a coach.

Personally, we find the models of the parent as coach and the parent as teacher-counselor closest to what we as parents actually want to do. In the family, where social interaction takes place

Principles and Practices 123

between husband and wife and parents and children, these two models seem appropriate. Furthermore, they fit well with parenting drawn from the teachings of Jesus and the Bible. We are the guides, encouragers, and lovers of our children.

Principles of Nurturing Children and Youth

We next offer several principles and practices that make for well developed children and youth, as well as happy families. We realize that it's not always easy to employ them; it requires a concerted effort on our part as parents. But if we put love to work in parent-child relationships, both benefit, making for a more happy family life.

1. From a Christian perspective, a critical ingredient is *unconditional love*. This kind of love was demonstrated by our Lord, Jesus Christ. Unconditional love means that even though we discipline our children when they "mess up" or willfully disobey, punishment is immediately followed by both a reasonable explanation of why they are being punished with reassurance that they are still loved.

When we were children and our parents reassured us when they punished us that they still loved us, we didn't believe it. But as we grew older we came to realize that they did indeed love us. And our children, hopefully, will come to the same conclusion. Eventually they will appreciate the parents who cared enough to discipline.

Although children are not aware of it, they actually crave and demand discipline when they test our limits and rules. It is reassuring to them when these rules are consistently enforced. They know they can count on the stability and consistency in love and discipline.

We need to realize early that to do a good job of parenting, we can't always worry about being liked. As one pediatrician put it, "No matter what you do as a parent, your children will not *always* like you!" It's best to follow intuitive feelings about what we know to be right, appropriate, and best for children—even when we emerge as villains. Despite our noblest efforts, at times some children reject their family's values and example to go their own way. In such cases our only recourse is to be there when needed, be supportive, and uphold them in our prayers.

2. In addition to unconditional love, parents need to *respect* their children—respect their feelings, their wishes for privacy, and their ideas. They are unique individuals, real people, and we should respect them as such. Furthermore, we should never deny or reject their feelings, no matter how they appear to us. When they insist that they feel a particular way, and we say they do not or should not feel that way, children interpret this as a form of rejection. They become confused and feel they are not understood or cared for.

At times, our children may generate some creative ideas that appear odd or inappropriate to us. Again, it is important to be accepting and open to these ideas, even if we do not agree. Then, if necessary, gently guide them into a more constructive path. Since children need to be encouraged in creativity, our support of ideas is important.

Dr. Ross Campbell (1977) reminds us that when we relate to our children they should be given the same undivided attention we expect from them.[2] Children will not be convinced that we are listening attentively if we keep one eye glued to the TV or have the newspaper held in front of our face as we say to them, "Go ahead, honey, I'm listening!" The golden rule is no more relevant than when we are dealing with our children and our wife or husband.

3. A third element that is needed in good child nurture is a sense of *trust*. Children need to know that their parents trust them. This does not mean, however, that parents should not check up on them. Quite the contrary. When they say they are going to a friend's home, or when they agree to do a chore about the house, we should occasionally make sure they are indeed at the friend's home, or that they did complete the task. In the case of the chore, checking up gives us an opportunity not only to see if

they have accomplished the task, but it also gives us an opportunity to praise them for a job well done. As we check on them, they develop trust in us, that we really *do* care about them.

Children need to earn our trust, just as we need to earn theirs. Recently a young lady, Adele, said that when she told her mother she was going to a friend's house her mother would occasionally call and ask, "May I speak to my daughter? I'd like her to buy a quart of milk on the way home from your place." Adele added, "Mom didn't really need the milk. She was just checking up on me." But interestingly enough, Adele was not complaining. Now that she is older and married, with a child of her own, she thanks God for a mother who cared enough to discipline—to check up. When her mother learned that she was trustworthy the calls stopped. And Adele did all that she could to keep her parents' trust. When she was out with her friends and changed her original plans, she would take time to call home to let her folks know about it. She did this, in part, because her parents always treated her with respect. They informed her when they were coming home later than planned or had changed their plans.

4. A fourth element that is equally crucial in nurturance is providing *time* from our busy schedules for our children. Much has been written about "quality" versus "quantity" time. Obviously time spent with a child can be either productive and profitable or unproductive and destructive to our children's growth.

Unfortunately, some parents who did not plan to have children, had them "accidentally." (Many of us were "accidental blessings!") Most parents welcome these unanticipated children and assume their responsibility joyfully, and thank God for them. Some parents, however, resent them as intrusions and take out their hostility on the youngsters, blaming them for frustrated plans. Parents who resent their children could profit from a period of therapy. But if they refuse to accept their responsibility or to get therapy, then working outside of the home often gives the child respite from a frustrated parent. In such cases a competent "sitter," or day care center may prove to be a God-send.

Today for financial and emotional reasons, many mothers, along with fathers, are employed full-time outside the home. Research has shown that children from homes where mothers work outside are normally just as well adjusted as those in which parents do not—*all things being equal.* In many cases all things are nearly equal, but in some cases this is not true. It is too early to tell what price children are paying for mothers who resume their careers when the youngest child is still under a year old. So much depends on the quality of the support system in the family, and the substitute caregiver. A great deal also depends on whether or not the mother actually does provide quality time in the precious few hours she has with her children. A mother who works outside the home will surely need the willing support of her husband to compensate for the time and energy she is giving to her job or career.

A mother who is a full-time homemaker may tend to take the time she spends with the children for granted, and not place much emphasis on positive interactions. Or, she may become preoccupied with the tasks and responsibilities of running a home, leaving little time for the children other than for disciplining and assigning chores or tasks.

There is something to be said for quality time.[3] Some parents make a point of doing something special with their children, often allotting a specific amount of time for each child. They may take them for a walk, play ball or some other activity, or take them to McDonald's. In addition, many parents are careful to attend sporting events, concerts, recitals, or dramatic productions in which their children are participating. But it is also important to reserve a definite block of time to talk—to communicate—with our children. And even more important, we need to take time to *listen* to what they have to say.

We need to make certain we are not rationalizing the entire matter of "quality" versus "quantity" time. We must honestly ask, "Am I giving *enough* time?" Quality with too little quantity can be quite damaging to children, as well as to parents who will miss the various stages of development in their children's lives. We can never recapture the precious years of childhood and youth. It is difficult, also, for children to overcome feelings of neglect and rejection if they receive too little attention from their parents. How tragic if a child ultimately concludes, "Mom and Dad seemed to care more about *things*—the car, job, house, sports, clubs, and even the church—than they did me!" Or "They showered me with gifts when what I really wanted was their time and attention!"

5. Another factor essential to good, open communication between parent and child is that we be *non-judgmental.* Too often youths complain that they do not have an opportunity to present their case or explain their situation. Their complaint is that before they explain they are "condemned." If we hope to keep the lines of communication open with our children, it's best to withhold judgment and provide a warm, friendly environment in which they feel free to speak.

How many times have we been pounced on in years past by our own parents or some other authority figure who did not take the time to listen? Remember how it felt? Break the cycle. Listen!

6. *Guidelines and rules* must be developed for children of all ages. This is a parental responsibility we cannot ignore. Although it's crucial to be open and receptive to our children, and to listen and talk things out with them, this does not mean that we throw out all rules and agree with them. After all, we are their parents, and we have the responsibility of nurturing them. Often we must say "no." Children and youth need guidance and direction, and this includes steering them away from those choices and experiences that we know will be harmful to them. We should establish "house rules" for them to live by.

Recently, we asked university students in a sociology class on juvenile delinquency to write an essay telling why they did *not* become delinquents. One reason they all gave was that their parents loved them and instructed them, provided guidelines and rules for them to live by, and enforced them!

Children and youth need instruction. That is one of the basic meanings of "discipline." They may not always tell us so. They may chafe and complain at times. But make no mistake, they feel more secure when they know what is expected of them. They want to know what the limits are—how far they can go. In these essays students also expressed gratitude that their parents cared enough to discipline them within a framework of unconditional love. And it was because of this love that they said, "I didn't get involved in delinquent acts because I knew it would hurt them, and bring shame on the family."

Interestingly enough, Manhattan psychoanalyst, Dr. Peter Blos, says that "parents should set limits, affirm their personal values, deny the 'clamor' for grown-up status, and refuse to be intimidated by charges of 'authoritarianism.'"

Naturally, as children and youth mature, they should be given increasing freedom to make their own decisions and choices. In discussions of issues, problems, and choices, we can explore the options available to them and the consequences of their choices. If we offer them choices, however, we need to be prepared to go along with them. Remember, though, that ultimately the buck stops with mom and dad, whom God has provided with the responsibility, knowledge, and wisdom to guide them.

It is especially important that parents agree on the rules and how discipline is to be administered. Children are clever. They are motivated by self-interest just as we are—only more so. They will play parent against parent. They know which one is the "soft touch." Parents need to keep in touch, supporting each other in discipline. When a child comes saying, "Mother said . . ." we can respond as fathers with, "Let me check with your mother and I'll get back to you." When we don't agree with a decision or an action of our spouse, unless it is a life-threatening situation, it's best to wait until we can speak with our spouse alone about the problem, rather than disagree or argue in the child's presence.

7. *Partiality* is often a problem, from both the children's

perspective and that of the parents. It is often said that fathers are partial to daughters while mothers are partial to sons. In most cases, however, parents are merely attempting to tailor love and discipline to the needs of each child. Nevertheless, in some cases parents are in fact being partial. Mothers, and especially fathers, need to be on guard against this. Unfortunately other children in the family misinterpret the difference as favoritism on their parents' part. Often the child who feels that way needs special help and understanding.

Parents unconsciously show partiality when they develop a special bond between themselves and one of the children who shares a special interest of the parent. For example, the dad who is enthusiastic about football develops a great sense of camaraderie with his athletic son. Or the mother who loves music gives a great deal of time and support to the child in the orchestra or band. As parents we can work to be evenhanded in allocating our time, care, and discipline, conferring with our spouse about our children's feelings and needs. Obviously, honest communication helps in many of these cases, but if the problems are too deep-seated, family counseling should to be sought.

8. It is important to build up children's *self-esteem*—their sense of self-worth. Charles H. Cooley coined the expression, "Looking Glass Self," suggesting that we receive our self-image from the way we interpret actions and responses of others to us. This looking glass process begins in infancy and continues throughout life. If we treat children with love and kindness, if we are fair in our dealings with them, this will convince them that they are people of worth. Conversely, if children's experience consists largely of being yelled at, rebuffed, and rejected in any area of life, their sense of self-worth will suffer.

It's crucial that parents praise children when they do things well. Also they need praise for their efforts, especially when they try and fail. As they accomplish a goal or finish a task, a word of commendation will go a long way toward keeping them productive, contributing, and achievement oriented.

When children fail at a task or fail to do what they and we think is proper, it is best not to make too much of it. Children know when they have failed or disappointed or hurt someone, and they are usually hurting and disappointed in themselves. We don't need to compound their sense of failure or their sense of guilt. Wounded children need understanding, encouragement, support, and reassurance. Hopefully, they will learn from their errors, put their mistakes behind them, and move ahead more wisely and carefully.

9. One practice that helps keep morale high, and the lines of communication open, is to hold *family council meetings* in which all freely participate. These may be held at fixed intervals of time, or as the need arises. Some parents find the natural setting after the evening meal a good time.

Another helpful idea is to have a family devotional time. Together the family can share a portion of Scripture, discuss its application to life, sing a song or two, and pray about the needs of family and friends. Worshiping together in this intimate way can bring family members closer together.

John De Santo, a Presbyterian pastor, makes a good point about solving family problems. Rather than living from crisis to crisis, he counsels families to deal with the little problems as they arise. In this way we keep the brush fires from getting out of hand and becoming forest fires. As we have often heard, "An ounce of prevention is worth a pound of cure."

10. Another way to shore up the family and make children feel as if they are a part of it, is to *trust them with responsibility*. Some parents pay their children to do chores about the home, such as keeping their room clean, and mowing the lawns. But children probably should not be paid for such tasks. If money is to be given, some suggest that it be handled in much the same way as the chores. The children are part of the family and are entitled to share in the financial aspects as well as the work. They should be asked to contribute to the family because they are a part of it. In the family each member must learn to share. Scripture teaches

that we should bear our own burden (load), as well as help bear the burdens of others (Galatians 6:2-4).

If parents can afford to give an allowance to teach children how to manage and budget money, well and good. They need to be given the same amount everytime so that they can learn to budget with a set amount. Of course, the amount will likely change as the child grows older. Also, children are to be taught the meaning of Christian stewardship early. Managing money from an allowance or earnings from a part-time or summer job, they learn to share and give. They do this not only because Christ commands us to, but out of a sense of compassion for the needy. Christ set the example, and we should follow in his steps.

There are several ways parents can help children develop a sense of responsibility and also improve their self-esteem. We can do this by teaching them the principle of deferred gratification, self-control and self-denial, and critical decision making.

It's not uncommon for parents who grew up in a family that had little more than the bare necessities to vow, "My children will never be denied the things they want, as I was!" Such parents often fail to realize that it was the very fact that they did not get everything they wanted that contributed to their healthy character and personality development. Because there were limited resources, they learned that we cannot have everthing we want in life. They learned to save money for things they really needed and wanted. Because their every whim was not instantly gratified, they learned to defer gratification, investing their resources of money, time, and skills to achieve some future goal that was more worthwhile. They learned, also, that they must deny themselves, as their parents before them did, in order that others in the family might have something they needed.

While we ought to provide adequately for our children, the last thing they need is an overindulgent parent. The world outside of the home certainly will not grant them their every wish! In the "real world" they are expected to act responsibly, work, and produce in order to be rewarded. To some extent, we must include that aspect of the world in our home environment to help prepare them to cope and be successful.

To deny our children the privilege of learning early that they must make choices—even choices between better and best—and that choices have long and short term consequences, is to rob them of a sense of responsibility that would enable them to develop their self-esteem. It's best not to deny them the sense of struggle, the opportunity to develop self-control, or the situations in which they must deny themselves. For these help to motivate us to work to meet our needs, and also develop in us a sense of self-esteem. The Spirit of God who indwells us gives us power not only to love, but also to exercise self-control and persevere (Romans 5:3-5; 2 Timothy 1:7).

11. While children learn from our instruction, they learn best from our *example*, as we model before them by word, behavior, gesture, and silence. The behaviors, beliefs, and values that we wish them to practice need to be lived out before them. Long before we become aware of it, our children have "caught" our way of speaking, our way of behaving, our way of life. They absorb it, almost as by osmosis. Thank God, they often know better than to emulate all of our ways. To their credit they sort out some of our undesirable traits.

In the home they learn how to utilize time, to formulate goals and achieve them, and how to treat their mother and father and other folks. They learn all of this from us! Because our children learn more from the behavior we exhibit than from the precepts we teach them, it's best to be open and honest with them.

Do we want them to share their concerns and problems? Then we should share some of ours with them. (We are assuming that they are adolescents and we will be selective in our sharing, sharing more as they age and mature.) Do we want them to apologize when they offend and wrong someone? Then we must ask their forgiveness or apologize when we wrong them. Do we want them to bring their friends home so that we might meet them?

Then we should invite our friends in to socialize also. Do we want them to care for the elderly, the poor, and the needy? Do we want them to respect people of all races, religions, and socioeconomic classes? Then we ought to demonstrate this by our conversations, our caring, and our sharing.

Do we want them to integrate their Christian faith, applying it to their daily lives? Then they need to see and hear us do this day by day. Do we want them to be active, constructive, participating, and contributing members of the church? Then they need to see us participate in the life of the Christian community.

While there are exceptions, whether we like it or not, children and youth generally reflect the lifestyle we model for them in the home, church, and community. Some may rebel for a time, but eventually most come back to openly embrace and appreciate the values we tried to share with them.

12. Finally, when our children reach the stage when they want to launch out on their own, either to pursue a vocation or go to college, we need to let them go.

Dobson refers to "letting go" as the final task in building self-esteem. He says, "Letting go is not an easy task, but good parenthood demands it."[4] When our children reach that point in life we have probably done all the molding and nurturing we can do. What they need now are parent-friends who will stand by them with encouragement and support, as well as with a good listening ear.

At college and university we often encounter students whose parents insist on trying to control their destiny, who want to push them into majoring in a subject that will prepare them for a career in which the students have no interest. While these young people love their parents, they resent the way the parents attempt to manipulate and dominate them. Often, because students do not share their parents' enthusiasm for a career, they do poorly academically. In some cases they even drop out of the university. As parents, we should respect our children's career choices. As long as they pursue an honorable vocation, we should rejoice, support them, and assure them of our blessings.

Parents Have Parents, Too

Until the time we left home and established our own families, our parents provided for us in every way. They nurtured us in childhood, guided us through the troubled period of adolescence, and supported us as we sorted out our chosen vocations. When we needed them, they were always there with love and understanding. They did not view their expenditure of money, time, and affection as a sacrifice. Our well-being was their primary concern.

As our own parents age, as their health inevitably begins to fail, they need our loving support and our friendship. We have an obligation of love. Love needs to be put to work with letters, phone calls, and visits. Too many aging parents have been neglected and virtually abandoned by their children who are "too busy" to visit or write or call. Scripture admonishes us: "Do not withhold good from those who deserve it, when it is in your power to act" (Proverbs 3:27); "Honor your father and your mother" (Exodus 20:12). Jesus' commant to visit the lonely, the sick and the needy begins with our own parents, for to deny them is to deny the faith (1 Timothy 5:8; Proverbs 23:22; Matthew 25:31-46).

Perhaps some of us did not come from good homes. Our parents may have met few of our needs. We may still have feelings of resentment and anger for injustices we experienced. These are not uncommon feelings. But it's best to deal with these and then, in Christian love, begin to interact again with our parents. If our home life was not good, we are still commanded as Christians to serve and care for our parents. God can certainly assist us, if we seek his help in prayer. But if the situation is particularly difficult, professional counseling can be helpful. If we put forth the effort, we will be the better for it.

Keep Laughter in the Home

If any famiıes ought to be happy, it should be Christian

Principles and Practices

familes. We are not bound to material things, for we affirm that relationships are more important (Luke 12:15). We realize that the way to glorify God is by using material and personal resources (our time and abilities) to provide for the well-being of our own family first, and then the needs of others (1 Timothy 5:8).

There is enough sorrow and sadness in the world. The home is to be a place where we do pleasant things together as a family, as well as with each other—parent with parent, child with child, and parents with children. Time flies by too rapidly. Before we know it our children are grown and gone, and they and we are left with our memories. Will they be pleasant ones? Will they be memories that bring joy to the heart? We alone can decide. Let's not allow our job, career, or some other time-stealer to cause us to be unfaithful to our family.

A good friend, Anne Rommel, recently recovered from radical cancer surgery. She vowed to God that when she recovered she would do all within her power to provide "happy memories" for her two sons and daughter to carry with them into adulthood. She wants her children to look back and remember the joy and laughter. With God's help she and her husband, John, are doing just that. And so should we.

Let's give flowers to the living! And let us express our love for each child, as well as for our wife or husband, by word and deed.

Keeping a Proper Prospective

Loyalty to our wife or husband is the last point we would like to reaffirm. All couples have their ups and downs, moments when communication is not going well, periods of disenchantment, times when we are under stress due to illness or other problems, and days when we seem to be out of sorts for a variety of reasons. During these periods there is a temptation to run from the problems and divert our energies and attention elsewhere. Some immerse themselves in their work or in a recreational activity or hobby.

During these periods of estrangement or alienation, some find other men or women who lend a listening ear, often resulting in an affair. Many others confide in their children, burdening them with their marital problems, complaining to them, "You know your father (or mother) is not the easiest person to live with! You know...." While confiding in children may relieve the parent's anxiety and tension temporarily, it is not the best way to cope with marital problems for several reasons.

First of all, children should not be exploited. They are not therapists. They are children. They are not mature enough to handle the role of counselor. Second, children should not be "brainwashed" by one parent or be forced to take sides. Third, and most important, it does not solve the communication problem the one parent has with the other. Finally, if one persists in identifying with the children in this way, as opposed to facing and resolving the problems one has with the spouse, when the children are gone the parent will be left at home with a spouse who has become a virtual stranger. Therefore, let the children remain *our* children, and let us work at keeping the lines of communication open with our marriage partner.

Again we stress that our first commitment is to God, the second to our wife or husband, and the third to our children. If we truly worship and serve God, we'll find that God will direct us through his Word to use our every effort to please our spouse. As a husband or wife we must never get so busy with the children or with our jobs or careers that we fail to reserve some special time for one another.

No matter how industrious we are, we will never get everything done. There will always be another chore, another day. Likewise, if we make a god of *money*—if we love it—*it* will surely destroy us. So let's not allow work outside or inside the home to tyrannize us. Instead, let us use money and things to meet each other's needs. And let us, also, set aside some time for expressions of love.

CHAPTER 9

INFIDELITY IN MARRIAGE
Push and Pull Factors

Since there is one divorce for every two marriages in the United States, the subject of fidelity, faithfulness, is a timely one. In the opening chapter of the book we mentioned that all marriages experience conflict, hardships, and stress. It's inevitable. But the crucial factor for marital stability and happiness is the way we handle these pressures. Some couples experience more than their share of tragedy and misfortune—the death of a loved one, catastrophic illness, financial reverses, wayward children—and yet manage to remain cheerful, composed, and positive in outlook. Others, however, who experience personal and family problems that are far less by comparison seem to come apart at the seams.

Kin Relationship with God Primary

One thing that makes the difference for many of the "survivor types" is the fact that they have a solid foundation of faith on which their marriages are built. As Christians their primary kin relationship is with God in Christ. They don't place other relationships before the one they have with God. They take seriously the biblical injunction, "You shall have no other gods before me."

Why do we stress this? When we keep God enthroned in our hearts we are likely to be obedient to God's commands and be guided by Christian principles in family interaction. And God's commandments deal primarily with our relationship with him, and secondarily with others. God's Word tells us *what* our life goals should be, as well as *how* we should go about achieving them. The Bible tells us how to express our love—how we should speak, when to be silent, and how we should behave toward our spouse, children, parents, and others. It commands us to be humble (not proud), to be forgiving (not unforgiving and vindictive), to be responsible (not unsympathetic and indifferent), and to be faithful (not unfaithful). If we walk in fellowship and obedience to our Lord it inevitably follows that we will better relate to those in our family.

By keeping our relationship with God primary, we enjoy the guidance of God's Spirit. The Spirit removes our fear and anxiety, and gives us the power to exercise self-control and put love to work in our relationships with others. And the Spirit helps us to use our gifts and abilities in constructive, edifying behaviors. In addition, walking in love enriches our marital relationships and enables us to grow in oneness. For "love builds up" (1 Corinthians 8:1). Love also enables us to overlook a multitude of faults, even as God in Christ overlooks ours.

Wife-Husband Love Bond

Now while our primary kin relationship must be a vertical one with God, our secondary relationship must be the horizontal one with our spouse. Jesus said, "Love God ... and love your neighbor ..." (Matthew 10:37; Mark 12:29-31). And our spouse, as Martin Luther said, is our nearest neighbor. Naturally our children, the fruit of our union, are part of the oneness we experience in the family. Just as we love all people as they have need, so as parents we love others in the family (spouse, children, and other kin) according to their need. Obviously in this connection we are speaking of *agapic* or self-giving love. We realize that we are writing about the ideal towards which we should strive.

We Marry Because We Have Needs

In the real world of married people, problems and conflict are part and parcel of the married and family experience. Men and women marry because each have needs which the other can satisfy. In this mutual relationship we strive to meet one another's needs for affection, companionship, social and financial security, creativity, Christian fellowship, and service to others. Most of us would also include the need for children. Inevitably, as husband and wife seek to meet each other's needs, as well as satisfy their own, differences of opinion and conflict occur. At this point our faith plays a significant part. A healthy faith in God and Christ clearly make a difference in meeting the needs of everyone in the family.

Because faith is so important, the first step to infidelity begins when we drift away from God, his Word, prayer, and the fellowship of the church. This is a common theme in the Bible. When Israel and the Christian church strayed from God, then discord, oppression, and other suffering resulted. We are not suggesting for a moment that *all* human sickness and hardship are the result of disobedience to God. While some are (for example, the higher incidence of cancer among those who smoke, and the job loss that results from absenteeism and poor performance), most are simply a part of the human condition. When we do not live by biblical principles that govern human interaction, our infidelity to God makes us more vulnerable to the temptation to be unfaithful to our spouse and children. It may sound like an oversimplification, *but it is true nonetheless*. When we walk in obedience to the teachings of Christ, we are more apt to meet each other's basic needs.

A faltering faith weakens our desire to meet the basic needs for which each of us married. When these needs are inadequately met, we are more vulnerable to the temptation to look elsewhere for satisfaction. We believe that when people turn aside from their covenanted relationship with their spouse and God it is a form of idolatry. Having an affair involves covetousness. Two classical biblical examples are Joseph and David. Whereas Joseph's vigilant faith enabled him to resist the temptation to commit adultery, David's laxness resulted not only in infidelity but also murder (Genesis 39:1-18; 2 Samuel 11—12).

"Spouse Surrogates"

What are some of the "spouse surrogates" (substitutes) that men and women turn to? We call them surrogates because husbands and wives turn to other activities, interests, and persons when they feel that their spouse has failed them. Oddly enough the list is legion. We mention a few of the most common: religion, alcohol/drugs, work, sports, hobbies, reading, TV, sleeping, clubs, and lodges.

It may seem odd that as Christians we should mention religion as a surrogate. But since our book is addressed especially to those who profess faith in Christ, we thought it appropriate to mention it.

Consider the apostle Paul's twofold caution. In 1 Corinthians 13, Paul warns those who confuse activities and dedication to the point of death with love. He says that even if we sacrifice ourselves—"give our bodies to be burned"—for others, but have not love, we "gain nothing." While Paul is specifically addressing the super zealot who attracts attention to self, rather than ministering out of genuine love, it illustrates well those who use religion as a spouse surrogate. Often zealous adults in the church spend endless hours in religious activities while the basic needs of their wife, husband, or children go unattended. We are reminded of Mrs. Jellyby in Charles Dickens' *Bleak House* who is consumed with passion for the needs of people in faraway Africa (Borrioboola Gha on the Niger River), but cares nothing about the material and emotional needs of her husband and children.[1] Paul also warns in another letter that to neglect one's spouse and children is tantamount to denying the faith. It constitutes infidelity of the most serious sort (1 Timothy 5:8).

But while some use religion as an escape, most Christians find that their faith enables them to be a more faithful and helpful marriage partner or parent. But "spouse surrogates" other than religion are more common. When we turn to these we are guilty of infidelity. Usually when husbands and wives turn to them, they do so in an attempt to escape what they regard as a poor or inadequate marital situation. While they have the option of confronting their spouse with the problem(s), they choose the easier way out—they turn to a surrogate to have their needs met.

Recently someone told of a small alligator that got into a swimming pond. Rather than removing the intruder that nibbled at them, they fed it. Unfortunately, this led to the growth of the beast who soon took over the pond, making it unfit for human use. Our "small problems" which we fail to resolve are like the alligator. Failing to resolve them allows them to feed and grow, and before we know it we have an unmanageable "beast" on our hands. The only sensible way to deal with communication problems is to communicate. Failing to do so means that we are allowing pride to stand in the way of marital growth and harmony, and the mushrooming conflict will serve as a push factor toward infidelity.

Change Is Constant

When we married we were alerted to the fact that marriage would require change, and that we would experience conflict and hardship along with peace and joy. We knew from past experience that growth, personal and corporate growth, does not come easy. We promised our spouse at the altar to be faithful "in good times and in bad" (or "for better or for worse, for richer or for poorer, and in sickness and in health"). Fortunately, at the time we did not know all that was in store for us. But then we closed the door on all others. We tore up our "little black date book" and we promised to be faithful through all that God and circumstances would send our way.

Prior to marriage, if we experienced conflict in a relationship, we may have moved on to another male or female friend. But all that is past. Now we have committed ourselves to building an in-depth relationship with the one we love and married. While we may be "prone to wander," we resist the temptation, just as we resist the temptation to "leave the God we love" to follow lesser gods.

The late Kenneth Foreman, a Professor of Theology, said, "I could never quite understand why I often got along better with other women than I did with my wife. Then I realized that I did not try to change them!" Keep in mind that most relationships that we have with others tend to be on a superficial level. They do not deal with substantive issues, with things that actually affect our lives. So long as we keep the conversation light, we get on fabulously with them. But when we deal with the "real stuff of life," with bread and butter issues, problems and conflicts inevitably arise.

Loyalty and Humility Essential

If we hope to develop and improve our marriage, we continue to commit ourselves to be faithful. This means being absolutely loyal. We do not complain to a third party, whether parent, brother, sister, or friend, about difficulties or problems we may have in communicating with our spouse. Instead we go directly to our spouse with our complaint. This direct method of resolving difference is clearly advocated by Christ (Matthew 18:15). If we cannot bring ourselves to share things with our spouse, the sensible course is to seek out the counsel of our minister or a professional counselor. Another biblical principle that is relevant here is that we who are strong should help the weak. And we are all weak in some area. Therefore, if we see a weakness in our spouse, we should not dwell on it, or ridicule or nag the other person. Our partner needs our understanding, support, and encouragement.

One of the basic virtues of the faith is humility. We are counseled not to be proud, but to remember that we too are frail, and that at one time or another we all fail and falter. Scripture admonishes us to submit to one another (Ephesians 5:21), to mutually serve one another out of love and in humility.

One Hundred Percent Commitment Necessary

The best safeguard is to make an irrevocable, one hundred

percent commitment to our spouse. Marriage dare not be a 50/50 proposition—we cannot be half dedicated to its success. Our commitment is to be an unconditional one. No matter what the circumstances or the response of the spouse, we stand firm in our commitment. Mutual submission and service are an integral part of this type of loyalty and dedication. Jesus modeled the servant role for us and, as his disciples, we are called to do the same in marriage. We do not keep score of the wrongs done to us, but unconditionally love and serve the other in a permanent relationship. The end result of such a commitment and relationship is both freedom and growth.

The power of an unconditional commitment was driven home recently by a statement made by one man who had been married three times. He admitted that he was not faithful to his two previous wives. When asked why he was faithful to his present wife, his third, he replied, "I just made up my mind that I would be! Oh, I have had chances to be unfaithful, and I have been tempted, but I haven't yielded." Such is the power of unconditional commitment. It serves as a hedge against infidelity.

Push Factors and Infidelity

Various *push* and *pull* factors are invariably correlated with infidelity. We conducted a survey of both men and women, asking them, "What factors within a marriage do you think *push* husbands and wives to be unfaithful, and what factors about our society *pull* them into infidelity?" The 30 people asked represented all strata of society.

By far, the most common response was that *poor communication* was the key push factor. Most believed that adultery was the result of a breakdown in communication, although a few mentioned that a spouse's refusal to be intimate was a strong push factor. As we mentioned in the earlier chapters on communication and conflict, there are numerous reasons why couples stop talking to one another. The important thing to realize, however, is that if one spouse stops talking—stops sharing things, planning, dreaming, sharing goals—there *are* reasons.

In some ways committing adultery is similar to becoming a juvenile delinquent. Most of them are not "pulled" into a life of crime; they are "pushed" into it from within the family. A young fellow does not suddenly blurt out, "I shall become a delinquent!" He usually drifts into it because his need for recognition and status are not being met at home. Since he is not receiving the positive strokes he craves, he adopts the lifestyle of those who grant him strokes. He wants to be "somebody." Husbands and wives have similar needs. So if we eliminate the push factor of poor communication we have taken a key preventive step against infidelity.

Another push factor is being unrealistic about our *expectations* of our wife or husband. (See chapter 3.) Several people mentioned the diabolical influence the mass media plays in shaping our lives. It has a way of squeezing us into its mold. "Madison Avenue" tells us what the good life consists of. It tells us what to wear, what to eat, and what car to drive. It also tells us what qualities a contemporary husband or wife should have—how we should define our gender roles in marriage. If we take our cues for behavior from the media, from the outside, we will always be at it's mercy. In addition, we will be vulnerable to exploitation. We will never have a marital relationship that is satisfying because it is not based on reality, but on media fantasy.

Change is a constant factor of life. It is an inevitable result of biological maturation and social and intellectual growth. But if we make the mistake of adopting the values and life goals the media dictates, we will never achieve stability and freedom in marriage. Our lives will constantly be changing to conform to the dictates of others. Only by guiding our lives by biblical precepts and principles can we be truly free, and yet find stability in changes we experience as we pass through the marital/family life cycle.

Contemporary society suffers from a state of anomie or normlessness. And unfortunately the Christian community does also. The church has been invaded by the world and has adopted its value system to a large extent. This places an unusual burden not only on the individual, but also on the married pair to sort things out for themselves. We must continually ask ourselves, "What are the Christian values we affirm?" and "What are the wordly or secular values that seek to undermine them?"

Not only do we get false expectations from the media, but we bring them into marriage from the experiences we had in our family of origin. While some of us may have been spoiled by overindulgent parents, others may have experienced rejection and abuse. Still others may have been the victim of an unusually dominant parent that caused them to vow, "No one is going to push me around!" Whatever the source of our unrealistic expectations, it is difficult to find satisfaction in marriage if we expect our spouse to change, conforming to the image we seek to impose.

We often have false and unrealistic expectations in many areas of life, but we soon learn to adjust our expectations to reality. So in marriage we must adjust—compromise, accommodate, and cooperate—for each others's well-being and that of the entire family. *We cannot always have things our own way!* As mature adults we must learn to put away childish ways and acknowledge that *we* do not live up to our spouse's expectations either! Realizing this should make it easier to accept our spouse as is. If any changing takes place it will come, not because we nag, harass, and apply sanctions. It will occur only as we personally demonstrate that change is possible—as we ourselves change to meet our partner's needs.

Still another push factor that follows from one spouse being spoiled, neglected, or abused, is the fact that such a spouse may not be willing to assume *a fair share responsibility* in marriage. When this happens the burden becomes unbearable for the responsible spouse, and it is only a matter of time before the person cracks under the strain or opts out of the marriage. While it is an overworked analogy, it is still one of the best and most applicable. Just as a team of horses cannot pull a wagon if each is determined to pull in a different direction, or if one refuses to move forward at all, neither can a couple advance harmoniously in marriage unless they have agreed on the direction they are heading and pull together. We need to agree on marital values and goals, and both be committed to pulling our own weight.

Boredom was yet another push factor that many cited. They complained that marriage had become humdrum. It lacked excitement! Stop and reflect. Remember how we planned activities before marriage that would please one another. We worked together not only at planning entertainment and recreational activities, but also on work projects. We helped one another. We supported one another. What has happened?

It is true that our circumstances have changed. We each have jobs and careers. We have children and all the responsibility that goes with them. We are involved in church and community affairs. But these very things can be the source of joint efforts that bring joy and satisfaction. We need not let them force us into a rut from which we cannot extricate ourselves. Both husband and wife need to rediscover each other. We need to save some of the quality time for each other. Wives often complain about boredom. Even if a wife elects to be homebound and to shoulder the primary responsibility of child care, nurturance, and guidance, she still needs social and creative outlets. Her social, mental, and spiritual well-being demands it.

When the extended family was stronger, when we usually lived in the same neighborhood, help in child rearing was readily available. With kinfolk all around, a great deal more socializing took place. Today, with all the geographical mobility, the nuclear family is often isolated from such a support network. While a good church may provide a substitute for the extended kin network, it probably cannot meet all of our needs. The burden really falls on the husband to work out a schedule that will free his wife to engage in creative, meaningful activities outside of the home. He will take the initiative to assist his wife with child care and household labor. If the husband does this, he will have eliminated, or at least softened, another push factor.

Pull Factors and Infidelity

In addition to the push factors cited above, the survey identified three pull factors. An important pull factor is *the extreme permissiveness of contemporary American society.* Our society no longer supports traditional Christian values—at least not to the same extent it did 40 years ago. We are living through a period of tremendously rapid social, technological, and economic change—a virtual revolution. (Those whose jobs have been eliminated by robots, automated machinery, or the movement of industry overseas are keenly aware of this!)

Whereas 40 years ago divorce carried a stigma, today it does not. In the past businesses and corporations frowned on divorce and viewed such persons as ill suited for promotion. The rationale seemed to be that if a man (and it usually was a man then) could not successfully manage his own marriage, how could he competently manage his responsibility for the firm? All that has now changed. Today, if a husband *or* wife obstructs a mate's progress in the firm, divorce is accepted as one legitimate solution to a dysfunctional marriage.

Even the Christian church has modified its rules (and theology) about divorce. In the past it took a firm stand against divorce, but now (whether appropriate or not) some of its most prominent leaders are divorced persons.

Peers, and especially the mass media, portray divorce as one effective way of coping with a bad marriage.

Living in a society that now offers *easy divorce* constitutes a powerful pull factor. One sees advertisements in the newspapers for $175 divorces, as well as "do it yourself" kits. Modern society emphasizes personal freedom and individual happiness above one's need to shoulder responsibility, endure a little pain, think of the common good, and accept conflict and stress as an integral part of life. This constitutes an even stronger pull factor.

We cannot turn the clock back. But those of us who profess to follow Christ can greatly reduce the pull factor of society's hedonistic philosophy by rededicating ourselves to the radical *agapic* ethic of Christ. By keeping our kin relationship with God and Christ fresh and vital, the power of the world's philosophy can be diffused. But more importantly, a logical consequence of our faith will be growth in love in the family as selflessness and servanthood (not selfishness and dominance), become our mutual goal.

Another pull factor that individuals (most often wives) cite is the desire to leave the marriage and *"go out there and find out 'who I am'!"* This has always appeared enigmatic to us. How can one find oneself by running away from responsibility? Some say, "I never had a chance to be my own person." Often these people have married early. But one only becomes one's own person when he/she assumes responsibility and lives responsibly. While we acknowledge that some marriages are best dissolved by divorce (especially in cases where there is flagrant infidelity and physical and psychological abuse), many of the people we have spoken to and counseled have found that they *did not* find themselves through divorce. Many, both husbands and wives, confessed that they merely substituted one set of problems for another. They reported that they would have been better off if they had stayed with their first spouse and worked harder at making the marriage work. It is important to work at mending broken fences, and rebuilding bridges of communication. Decide that growth will be an inward experience—personally and as a couple.

Often when communication is poor, drastic steps may be necessary to bring about a change in the relationship. Sometimes it works, and sometimes it doesn't. One Christian wife who endured years of abuse at the hands of an alcoholic husband finally issued him an ultimatum, "Get help or I'm leaving!" He got help! Through joint therapy they are now rebuilding their marriage. Both found themselves because one cared enough—loved enough—to confront. Love does include justice! It is not fair to the abusing spouse to allow him or her to get away with irresponsible behavior.

A third pull factor that goes along simultaneously with the push factor of poor communication is *the recognition and strokes one receives from outside of an unsatisfying marriage*—on the job, in one's career, through activity in a civic club, through a hobby, or in religious activity. Human beings like to receive recognition. We want people to pat us on the back and say, "You've done a fine job!" We want to be loved and wanted. We try to avoid painful situations. If we find life at home unsatisfying, if our contribution goes unappreciated and unrewarded, if our self-esteem suffers—we seek other outlets. The husband who is a workaholic, for whatever reason, and neglects his wife's need for companionship will find that she will seek to have this need met in some other way, either through the children or a relative, or someone else. Often companionship is found through work or service outside of the home. Therefore, his infidelity (neglect) may make her vulnerable and receptive to the affirmation of another. On the other hand, a busy wife may neglect the needs of her husband.

Adultery Does Happen . . .

Finally, we would like to deal more fully with the problem of adultery. We noted earlier that this is not usually the root cause, but rather the consequence of poor communication or the result of one's needs not being met. And the need for physical intimacy is one of those needs!

There are, however, those who are unfaithful for other reasons. Sometimes a spouse is insecure and is seeking to bolster a poor self-image by having affairs with others. In this way a spouse can be reassured that he or she still has "it" (whatever "it" may be). This is often associated with the mid-life crisis men often go through, although some experience it long before mid-life.

One may have an affair to punish a spouse for some slight in their relationship. Or one may drift carelessly into an affair. While a friendship may begin innocently, eventually it gets out of control.

But, for the most part, sexual infidelity is the consequence of neglect and poor communication. For example, a new mother may neglect her husband when a child comes into the family. She may not involve him in child-care, or she may become so preoccupied with the child that she has no time for him. Rather than confronting her with his sense of alienation and isolation, he may seek to have his needs met by another woman. Or he may turn to a spouse surrogate activity in which he finds satisfaction. (He may have tried to call his wife's attention to his needs and been rebuffed and labeled as "selfish" and "inconsiderate.") On the other hand, a husband may become so involved in his work or avocation that he forgets that his wife has needs, and his neglect may push her out to find satisfaction elsewhere.

We offer a word of caution again. When communication is faltering, punishing a spouse by denying affectional needs only compounds the communication problem. Sexual rejection is interpreted as just another indication that one is not loved. However, when the couple continues physical intimacy while persistently ignoring the underlying problem, they are inviting disaster. As one male put it, "While sex may be the frosting on the cake, there is just so much frosting one can take without getting sick." The answer is to be found in restoring some substance to the relationship. Then the frosting will have more meaning. As mentioned in a previous chapter, sex is no substitute for genuine intimacy that emerges from good communication.

Handling Infidelity

What do we do when our spouse is unfaithful to us? There are several options.

1. *Repentance, Forgiveness, and Reconciliation.* The offending spouse should sincerely apologize (repent) and seek the forgiveness of the other. We should honestly accept the fact that given certain circumstances and situations, each of us might be guilty of infidelity. (Remember, pride usually goes before a fall!) The essence of the Christian gospel is forgiveness, a manifestation of Christian *agape* love. The Old Testament stresses that God is compassionate, merciful, and forgiving, and the New Testament

emphasizes that we are forgiven and reconciled to God solely by grace, by God's redemptive act in Christ. Since God forgives us freely, and since *all* of us fail and falter in some way at some time, God calls on us to be forgiving, as God has forgiven us. If we expect God to forgive us our sins, we must forgive others (see the parable of the unforgiving servant—Matthew 18:21-35). There is no room for pride and self-righteousness.

If we have committed adultery, the best course of action is to level with our wife or husband. While this will undoubtedly be painful, we must bear it bravely to achieve the goal of an effective reconciliation and healing in our marriage. We should *not* try to rationalize and justify our action or blame others for our infidelity. While there may be many reasons, there is really no excuse! There is no way around the pain and anguish, but after some time elapses, healing will take place. God and time are great healers.

If the repentance is genuine, certain behaviors inevitably follow. First of all, repentance is authenticated by a change of behavior. The word repent in Greek literally means to "do an about face"—to stop moving in one direction and go in the opposite direction.

So the first sign of genuine repentance will be severing our relationship with the "other person" or "third party." Just as the alcoholic must stop drinking before attacking the conflict and problems that push him or her toward alcoholism, so the unfaithful spouse must sever ties with the "other person" before trying to resolve the conflicts and problems.

The second sign of true repentance is that both partners put love to work by seeking to remove the barriers that each believes have caused the breakdown in communication and understanding. Often it is wise to seek the help of a trained counselor. It is best to avoid resorting to friends for help because friends are usually partial—they cannot be objective.

A third sign of genuine repentance and forgiveness will be evident when both partners work diligently and spend time together. Edward E. Ford suggests that it is best to engage in an activity together—going for a walk, playing tennis or Scrabble—rather than merely engaging in a spectator event such as watching TV or going to a movie.[2] Joint participation increases understanding and strengthens the bond between a couple.

Furthermore, each should realize that it takes time to heal a broken or fragile relationship. Just as the infidelity was the result of a long period of faulty communication, it will take some time to heal the relationship. While God forgives and forgets, remember that we are not God! The offended spouse is not perfect, as God is, and therefore the penitent spouse needs to be patient and empathetic. A little role reversal might help us understand the offended spouse's feelings.

2. *Brief Separation.* A second alternative to forgiving and working at reconciliation is separating for a brief time. Sometimes a cooling off period helps. It gives both spouses time to reflect, do some self-examination, pray, and possibly seek counseling.

3. *Divorce?* A third alternative is to forgive, but divorce. We believe that people rush into this option prematurely. Most people, *if* honest and open, *if* willing to humble themselves and admit that there is not an "absolutely innocent partner," and *if* willing to set aside pride, can resolve most problems. We realize this takes a monumental effort on the part of both, but it is possible to bring about a reconciliation and a healing. But sometimes the situation has deteriorated to such an extent that one spouse may be unwilling to repent or forgive, or the abuse may be so unbearable, that divorce is the best for all concerned.

As Christians, we must remember that each of us has a responsibility to work for the common good of the entire family. Especially when children are involved, irreparable damage is often done when pride and stubborness keep one from repentance and forgiveness—from compromising and accommodating to differences.

While the husband and wife may feel that they have a choice (to stay together or divorce), the children have no such choice. Both authors have worked with students and counseled with couples in which the children have been devastated by the divorce. Often they bear a sense of guilt for the divorce—a feeling of responsibility with which they should never have been saddled. Happiness, after all, is a relative thing. We urge alienated couples to pursue it. As the title of our book suggests, if love is put to work, relative happiness and harmony can be achieved. If both seek forgiveness and healing, they can overcome. With God's help all things are possible.

The Faithful Spouse

As we have seen a variety of push and pull factors affect fidelity in marriage. Positively stated, we will not be tempted to be unfaithful if we put love to work in marriage—

- By keeping our primary kin relationship with God and Christ vital, communing with God daily through prayer and Scripture reading, and staying actively involved in the church.
- By keeping the lines of communication with our spouse and children open.
- By facing problems and conflicts as they arise—head-on—and resolving them.
- By being loyal to our spouse—not turning to spouse surrogates for companionship and affirmation (whether it be our children, another adult, or an activity).
- By sharing with our spouse in *all* areas of life—not compartmentalizing or keeping our spouse "on hold" because we are not communicating well and are seeking satisfaction elsewhere.
- By being willing to endure the temporary discomfort we experience when we confront our spouse in an effort to eliminate those barriers that inevitably arise when conflicts are not resolved.
- By being mature and realizing that we cannot always have things our way.
- By being humble and playing the servant role as Jesus did.
- By realizing that we are often wrong, and the source of the problem; by being big enough to admit that when we are wrong we will ask for forgiveness and be reconciled.

◦ ◦ ◦

Greater love has no husband or wife than this, that they each demonstrate genuine care for each other daily in word and deed. Love is the most powerful force in the world. Let us put it to work for us in marriage!

NOTES

Chapter 1. Suffering in Marriage

1. The teachings of Christ not only serve as a guide for personal living, but also for marital and family relationships. One of Christ's basic teachings is that discipleship demands obedience, and this includes suffering. Christ said that the road is *hard* (Matthew 7:12-13), that we must bear his *yoke* (Matthew 11:29), and that we must carry a *cross* daily (Luke 9:23). He also said that we will experience *trials* and *tribulations* in the world (John 16:33). It is by being obedient and by accepting the suffering that discipleship involves that we find God's grace, strength, and peace. The apostles also make it clear that the Christian life includes suffering. Check out Romans 5:3-5; 8:17-18; 2 Corinthians 1:5-7; Philippians 3:10; 1 Thessalonians 3:3-4; Philippians 1:29; 2 Timothy 3:12; 1 Peter 2:20-24; 4:16-19; James 1:2-4, 12; and Hebrews 2:10; 11:1—12:11.

2. M. Scott Peck, *The Road Less Traveled*, Touchstone Book 5, 1980, see chap. 1.

3. Joseph and Lois Bird, *Marriage Is for Grownups*, Image Books, 1971

Chapter 2. Religion in Marriage

1. M. Scott Peck, chapter on "Growth and Religion," in *The Road Less Traveled*.

2. William L. Smith-Hinds, "Sources of Knowledge," in *Reader in Sociology: Christian Perspectives*, edited by C. P. De Santo, et al., Herald Press, 1980.

3. Robert Cole, "Lay a Solid Religious Foundation for Your Children," *Family Weekly*, July 15, 1984.

4. See C. S. Lewis, *Mere Christianity*, Macmillan, 1964; G. K. Chesterton, *Orthodoxy*, Greenwood, (1909) 1974; and Anthony Campolo, *A Reasonable Faith*, Word, 1985.

5. William Barclay, *The Letters to the Galatians and Ephesians* (Second Edition), Westminster Press, 1976.

Chapter 3. Expectations in Marriage

1. John F. Crosby, *Illusion and Disillusion: The Self in Love and Marriage*, (Third Brief Edition), Wadsworth, 1984.

Chapter 4. Love in Marriage

1. M. Scott Peck, chapter on "Love" in *The Road Less Traveled*.

2. *Journal of the Pennsylvania Medical Society*.

3. Judson Swihart, *How Do I Say I Love You?* InterVarsity Press, 1977.

4. John S. J. Powell, *The Christian Vision*, Argus Communications, 1984. See especially chapter 4, "The Christian Vision of Self." See also James Dobson, *Hide or Seek*, Fleming H. Revell Co., 1981. For a critique of self-esteem emphasis, see W. K. Kilpatrick, *Psychological Seduction: The Failure of Modern Psychology*, Thomas Nelson, 1983, and *The Christian's Self-Image: Issues and Implications*, Wayne Joosse, Calvin College, 1987.

Chapter 5. Communication in Marriage
   1. Sven Wahbroos, *Family Communication*, (Revised Edition), A Plume Book, 1974.
   2. John Scanzoni, *Sexual Bargaining* (Second Edition), The University of Chicago Press, 1982.

Chapter 6. Conflict and Anger in Marriage
   1. George Hillery, Jr., "A Christian Perspective on Sociology," in *Reader in Sociology: Christian Perspectives*, Edited by C. P. De Santo, et al., Herald Press, 1980.
   2. *Ibid.*

Chapter 8. Child Rearing in Marriage
   1. Mary A. Lamanna and Agnes Riedmann, *Marriages and Families*, (Second Edition), Wadsworth, 1985.
   2. Ross Campbell, *How to Really Love Your Child*, Signet Books, 1977.
   3. Zig Ziglar, *Raising Positive Kids in a Negative World*, Oliver Nelson, 1985.
   4. James Dobson, *Hide or Seek*, revised edition, Fleming H. Revell, 1979.

Chapter 9. Infidelity in Marriage
   1. Charles Dickens, *Bleak House*, (1953) 1970.
   2. Edward Ford and Steven L. Englund, *Permanent Love*, Winston Press, 1979.

STUDY AND DISCUSSION QUESTIONS

Chapter 1. *Suffering in Marriage: Minimizing the Stress*
1. The authors say that all marriages involve "suffering"; that is, all couples experience constraints, stress, and strains as well as problems and disappointments. Do you agree? What has been your experience?

2. What sorts of problems and difficulties do you think are common to most marriages?

3. How do you relate Romans 5:3-4, where Paul writes about suffering in the Christian's life, to marital relationships?

4. How does modern romantic love differ from the Christian concept of agape love? See John 3:16; 13:34-35; 1 John 4:7-11, 19-21. How do these verses apply to marital and family relationships?

5. How does the case of Troy and Beth illustrate the true nature of agape love?

Basic Beliefs of Our Faith
6. In what areas have you tried to take over those tasks that your spouse should rightfully assume, depriving your partner of personal growth and development?

7. Do you agree that each of us is the only one who can make ourselves happy? How do we go about doing this?

8. In what ways does Galatians 6:2-5 relate to carrying your own load and also to assisting your spouse when your partner needs help?

9. How does the case of Larry and Grace point up our responsibility to facilitate the growth of our spouse? Can you think of other things that we can do to help our spouse feel fulfilled?

10. Do you agree with the authors that "we can do too much" for our spouse? How does this diminish the growth of a husband or wife or both?

Why Do We Have Conflict?
11. Most people fantasize about a conflict-free marriage. What three sources of marital conflict do the authors suggest? Can you think of other causes? How do verses such as James 3:2a; 2 Corinthians 13:12; Matthew 7:13-14; 11:29a; Philippians 2:12-13; Proverbs 16:18; 29:23a; and Romans 12:3 enlighten our understanding of the sources of conflict?

12. In what ways do you see pride contributing to Tom's folly? How has pride kept you from communicating and solving problems in your marriage? How can we prevent pride from giving us a false impression of our self-worth? (See Romans 12:3; Matthew 7:1-5.)

13. Where in our relationships can we demonstrate the fruit of the Spirit? Be as specific as possible.

Being Aware of Our Beliefs
14. What four false notions do the authors suggest that we should get rid of? Are there others you would add?

15. Have you ever fantasized about a perfect marriage? What were the elements of your fantasy? What hindered their realization?

16. Give your marriage a checkup. Can you identify and share some of the things you and your spouse have been doing right? What have you and your spouse failed to do that needs to be done? What are your present goals—short-term as well as long-term? In what way are they different because you are a Christian?

Eliminate the Negative
17. Give some reasons why you think comparing your marriage with others is not helpful? What can we learn from observing other marriages and families in their interaction?

18. Why do you think the authors believe "blaming others" is unprofitable?

19. Are you contemplating "what might have been" in some areas of your marriage? Is there any redeeming value in such thought?

Study and Discussion Questions

20. Why are "if only" statements and speculating about marriage to another person pointless and harmful to a marriage? How might we eliminate such thoughts? Do you agree with John Giles statement about "it's now or never"?

21. What are the good qualities that first attracted you to your spouse? What are the good qualities of your partner that you have discovered since you've been married?

22. Do you agree with the authors when they say that marriages need to be renewed and nurtured to grow? What are the alternatives to growth and renewal?

23. Why does a change in behavior result in a change in attitude? Why does a change of attitude also result in changed behavior? Analyze the change that took place in the prodigal son (in Luke 15), as well as the failure of the elder brother to change. How can we relate these insights to our life within marriage and the family?

Chapter 2. *Religion in Marriage: Believing the "Right Stuff"*
Behavior Reveals Beliefs

1. Do you agree that our religion, which is really composed of our beliefs about all reality, is reflected in our words and deeds? What evidence can you give for such an assumption?
2. What does Jesus say about the relationship between heart and behavior, words and deeds? Consider Matthew 12:33-37; compare it with Galatians 5:19-24.
3. What is your religion? That is, what is the set of beliefs about reality that constitutes the driving force in your life? Are your spouse's beliefs similar/different from yours? Discuss ways you have gone about harmonizing and modifying your differences.

Healthy Religion

4. Why are the basic beliefs of spouses crucial to healthy marriage and family interaction? Discuss ways these beliefs apply practically to relationships within the family. In what ways do you see God's judgment as a part of love in the case of Don?
5. Active faith is authentic faith. What does God expect of us when we profess faith in him? Consider: Micah 6:8; Matthew 7:12; Mark 12:29-31; Matthew 5:13-16; Romans 12:1-21; 1 Corinthians 13:1-13; James 2:15-17; and John 13:1-18. Are there other key Scripture passages you would add? How do these relate to marital and family relationships?

Christ and Forgiveness

6. Christianity is a religion that emphasizes God's grace—his unmerited favor toward us. Christ emphasized forgiveness, as do the apostle's in their writings in the New Testament. See Matthew 6:12; 18:15-35; Mark 11:25-26; 2 Corinthians 2:7; Ephesians 4:32; and 1 John 1:9. What are some of the things for which we need to forgive our spouse and children? How about things for which they need to forgive us?
7. In what ways did pride prove to be destructive to Kevin's marriage? How can we prevent the destructiveness of pride from interfering in our personal lives and in our marriage?

An Attitude of Gratitude

8. Give some thought to what you have for which you are grateful. List things you are grateful for about your spouse and children. How does a grateful attitude keep a person and a marriage from going sour?

Love and Justice

9. How do you relate Luke 17:3-4 to the concepts of love and justice (or "tough love") wherein we confront our spouse or others with an offending behavior? In what ways are love and justice related in the case of Jay and Ruth?

Christ's Teaching About Oneness

10. What James Dobson calls "tough love" the authors call justice. In what ways is justice an integral part of love?
11. Is there any present interest of your spouse that you need to be putting first? What does it mean to put this interest of your spouse first? What does it mean to put this interest first? Would it improve your relationship?

The Patriarchal Emphasis

12. It is the authors' belief that the emphasis in Christian marriages should be on love and servanthood, mutual submission or supportiveness, as well as on the oneness of the husband and wife who constitute the head of the family. While they recognize the patriarchal tradition of Paul, they believe that Christ's teaching should take precedence over Paul's. What is your belief about headship in the family, and what biblical or other evidence do you use to support your beliefs? Check out these references on "oneness" and "mutual submission": Mark 10:6-9, 42-45; John 13:12-16; Ephesians 5:21; and 1 Corinthians 7:4. For the patriarchal idea of the husband as the head, see Ephesians 5:22-33; Colossians 3:18-19; 1 Corinthians 11:1-3; and 1 Peter 3:1-2.

Study and Discussion Questions

13. How do you feel about the idea of mutual submission or supportiveness? How do Jesus' teachings on servanthood apply to marriage?

Commitment Means Something!
14. What does commitment mean in your marriage?
15. How does commitment serve as a deterrent to divorce?
16. Do you agree with the authors when they state that commitment would enable us to concentrate on resolving differences, rather than allow differences to disrupt a marriage? Why do you think commitment would serve as a deterrent to separation and divorce?

Chapter 3. *Expectations in Marriage: Adjusting to Reality*
1. Referring to the list of expectations in the beginning of the chapter, identify those you had before marriage. Did you have others?

There Is Always a Gap
2. Is there always a difference between the real and ideal?
3. If we make adjustments to the reality of the situation in other areas of life, why do you think we have difficulty adjusting to the reality of the married experience?

The Expectations Gap
4. Are there any persistent gaps today between your expectations and the reality of your marriage?
5. What happened to the expectations once you were married? What adjustments did you and your spouse make to the reality of life circumstances in your marriage? What positive experiences and traits did you experience that neither of you expected?

Society's Influence
6. What values do we emphasize in Western society?
7. Are they detrimental to the individual, marriage, and the family? When? Under what circumstances? How do you as a Christian modify and adapt or reject any of these values?

The Family's Influence
8. What expectations, traits, and/or behaviors did you inherit and learn from your family? What expectations, traits, and/or behaviors do you see in your spouse that came from his or her family?
9. What *new* expectations, traits, and/or behaviors have you developed since you married? In Philippians 3:13 Paul talks about forgetting the past. In 2 Corinthians 5:17 he mentions "becoming a new creation" in Christ. In Romans 12:1-2 he speaks of the need to strive to be transformed. How do these ideas relate to bringing marital ex-

pectations into line with ideas of growth into oneness, as well as growth in the Christian faith?
10. Can you share with the group any negative traits which you have eliminated from among those you learned within your parents' family?
11. How did your parents' use of money prepare you to handle money in marriage?
12. Was your sex education adequate preparation for marriage? In what ways did you add to or subtract from the nurture you received?

Peer Influence
13. How did your peer experience prior to marriage influence your marital expectations? What adjustments have you had to make now that you're experiencing marriage?
14. Would you say that peers still influence you? In what ways?
15. In what ways do your Christian friends serve as both your reference group and your peer group?

Media Influence
16. The influence of TV, radio, magazines, and newspapers are often subtle but pervasive. How has the media, especially TV, influenced your marital expectations? What shows do you consider particularly influential—for good or ill? What shows influence what you expect in and from marriage?
17. Were there any songs during your youth and courtship days that may have influenced your expectations? What lyrics from these songs come to mind?
18. Do you see evidence that the TV catechism exists? Are there values TV teaches that the authors have missed? What positive values has TV reinforced?

The Women's Rights Movement
19. No one can deny that the women's rights movement has exerted a great deal of influence on both men's and women's roles today. How has the movement influenced your marriage? What changes have taken place in your marital roles?
20. What positive and negative changes can you identify in marriage and in society as a result of the movement? Do you see women and wives as experiencing greater self-fulfillment today? What factors create problems and conflict for men and women as a result of the women's movement?

False Expectations and the Church
21. Have you felt pressure from your church's teachings to have a "perfect marriage?"

Study and Discussion Questions

22. Undoubtedly your church has offered positive help and guidance to those who are married and have families. Can you identify specific examples?

To the Remarried
23. In what ways can those who have remarried profit from a past failure?
24. If you have remarried, what tips or counsel can you offer to others (single, married) that will help improve their marriage?

Expectations, Reality, and Love
25. Discuss the merit of the authors' notion that in all other areas of life we make adjustment to reality, and therefore we shouldn't be surprised when we have to make adjustments in marriage.
26. Do you agree with the authors' assertion that the first step to making marriages happier must begin by each of the couples making themselves happier by living responsibly? Why? Why not? Discuss.

Chapter 4. *Love in Marriage: A Way of Behaving*
Meaning of Love
1. How do you define love?

Love Is Not an Emotion
2. What emotions do you associate with love? Are these feelings always pleasant ones?
3. In what ways do you demonstrate love that are not accompanied by "happy" feelings? Be specific.
4. Examine the case of Jane and Russ. Does the lack of evidence of love mean that there is *no* love?
5. Have you ever changed your behavior (from negative or passive to positive) and noticed your attitude also changed? Have you ever done this in love for your spouse? Share as many such experiences as you can.
6. Although the romantic "high" of courtship may be gone in your marriage, romance is still important. How have you worked at keeping romance in your marriage? What can we learn from the quote from the *Pennsylvania Medical Society Journal* and the one from *My Fair Lady*?
7. In what ways can a husband and/or wife go about deepening their love for each other?

An Unconditional Commitment
8. Why is unconditional love important to a marriage?
9. How has your love commitment to your spouse sustained your marriage?

Love Can Grow
10. Are there some areas of your life in which you feel you are acting in a self-centered manner? How could these behaviors be changed to other-centered ones?

Love's Many Expressions
11. What are some of the ways a husband and wife can show love for each other?
12. Why are words not enough? Examine the case of the couple in graduate school.

Measuring Love
13. As you read 1 Corinthians 13:4-8a, which aspects of love do you possess and which show little evidence in your life?
14. What spiritual exercises have you found helpful in perfecting your love?

Wisdom in Marriage
15. Why do the authors insist that wisdom must be coupled with the expression of love? See James 1:5 and 1:19.
16. What are occasions when silence and inaction are more loving than words or deeds?
17. Why do you think we are more impatient with our spouse's shortcomings than we are with our own? What is God's attitude toward his children's imperfections? See Matthew 18:23-35; 2 Peter 3:9; Psalms 103:3-4; and Isaiah 42:3a.

Confronting in Love
18. Confronting someone with his or her faults or harmful behavior is always difficult. No one enjoys being corrected. But Paul urges us to "speak the truth in love" (Ephesians 4:15). Can we truly love our spouse (or child) if we fail to correct them when they are doing something that is harmful to themselves and others.
19. Discuss Dr. Hopple's point about accentuating the positive. Why does it pay off more in the long run?
20. Discuss how Matthew 18:15-17 and 1 Peter 1:22 apply to family relationships.
21. What new insights could we gain by role reversal—changing places with our spouse?

Expressing Love
22. How does your spouse show his or her love for you? How would you like to have it expressed? If these are different, why not tell your spouse how you prefer to have love expressed? Are you certain that

you are expressing love the way your spouse would like? If you don't know, what's the best way to find out?
23. Think about the concept of reciprocity—that we express love for one another in different ways at different times. Can this idea help us show love, even though we may not be keen about it?
24. Why doesn't love eliminate conflict? How does love help us resolve or manage conflict?

Love of Self
25. God loves you. Do you have a healthy self-love? If not, how can you go about developing this and nurturing it?
26. How is Christian growth related to growth of self-esteem? Discuss Hebrews 6:1-4; Philippians 3:12-14; John 13:34-35; 14:15, 23; and Mark 12:30-31 as related to self-esteem.

Four Relationships
27. The authors realize that there are times when the needs of children take priority over the needs of one's spouse. Nevertheless they believe your spouse should come first. What do you think they mean by this? Could this be detrimental to a marriage? Do you know of marriages in which children have been neglected because priority was given to a spouse? Do you know of marriages in which a spouse is being neglected because priority is being given to the children?

Chapter 5. *Communication in Marriage: The Key to Growth and Happiness*
1. What power structure exists in your marriage: (a) Owner/Property, (b) Head/Complement, (c) Senior Partner/Junior Partner, (d) Equal Partner/Equal Partner?
2. Which ones do you think are consistent with Christian principles? Why?
3. Why is it important to agree on basics—authority structure, husband/wife role definitions, goals? How does this relate to communication and conflict?
4. What personality and temperamental differences between men and women can you identify? How do these affect a couple's communication pattern?

Communication with God
5. Why should communication with God take priority and precedence over communication with others? What benefits do we derive from communication with God?
6. Discuss the insidious ways pride obstructs honest, open communication.

Reasons We Do Not Communicate Well
7. The authors cite fear, early nurture in our family of origin, and feelings of insecurity as reasons why we do not communicate well with our spouse. Can you think of others? What keeps you from openly sharing with your spouse?
8. How many of the hindrances mentioned obstruct good communication in your marriage? How can you work to remove them? Be as specific as you can.
9. In what ways does fear hinder us from freely sharing feelings and ideas with our spouse?

Rules for Good Communication
10. The authors mention six rules for good communication. What are they? Which do you have the toughest time employing?
11. Have you had experiences similar to the "donut incident"? How can incidents like that be avoided?
12. In what ways does reflective listening help the communication process?
13. In what ways does talking about how we communicate with our spouse help marital communication?
14. Has your communication with your spouse improved over time? Share with the group what you have done to strengthen it.

Chapter 6. *Conflict and Anger in Marriage: Resolution and Management*
Root Causes of Conflict
1. Discuss the four root causes of conflict mentioned by the authors. Do you see them as fundamental causes? Can you add others?
2. All couples "fight" about some things. What are some of the areas that most have trouble with?

Barriers to Conflict Resolution
3. What are the six barriers to conflict resolution discussed by the authors? Which do you think are most harmful and why?
4. Why is it unwise to get sidetracked in arguments on peripheral issues and not acknowledge and deal with the real problem?
5. Why isn't temporary "peace" worth avoidance of the real problem?

Steps of Conflict Resolution
6. What are the six steps to conflict resolution? How do these differ from the way you go about resolving conflict?
7. Share with the group an example of how momentary pain yielded long-term gains.

Anger Can Be Controlled
8. All of us get angry. Some get loud, while others speak softly when angry. How have you dealt successfully with anger? Are there other steps that we might take to control or manage anger?
9. How does anger serve as a constructive force in marriage?
10. What instruction does the Bible provide in Proverbs 15:1, 4, 18; 29:11; Ephesians 4:26, 31; 2 Timothy 1:7 (RSV); and James 1:19-20 about controlling our temper and anger?

Work at Conflict Resolution When Not Angry
11. What do you do when you cannot resolve a conflict? How do you manage it?
12. How does Ephesians 5:21 and 1 Corinthians 8:13 apply to an impasse that does not concern a moral issue?

Chapter 7. *Sex in Marriage: An Act of Love*
1. What part do you think sexual intimacy plays in marriage? The Bible teaches that sex is good and vital to a good marriage. When God made us, he created us as sexual beings. Christ blessed the marriage in Cana of Galilee (John 2). Discuss the importance of sex in marriage in the light of Proverbs 5:15-23; 1 Corinthians 7:2-5; and Song of Solomon 4:1ff.

Affectional Needs Renewed Daily
2. In what ways does the Christian perspective on sex in marriage differ from a secular view?
3. Do you agree with the statement: "Our appetite for affection and sexual love is renewable each day." If so, why is it true? How can we go about resolving differences in expressed need?
4. What part can communicating with your spouse about sexual needs and difficulties do to help improve affection in marriage?
5. Think again about Proverbs 5:15-23 and 1 Corinthians 7:2-5. What guidelines can you come up with relative to sexual intimacy?

Sex Will Not Solve Communication Problems
6. Why won't sexual intimacy, per se, solve communication and other problems in marriage?
7. Why do the authors say that sex should not ordinarily be denied a spouse? Why the apparent contradiction with question six above?

Sex Drives and Desires Vary
8. Do you know what your spouse desires in the area of sexual affection? Does your spouse know what you desire? What is it that you would like in your affectional relationships that is not there now? What aspects would you like to eliminate?

9. In your experience, and from what you have read and learned from other sources, how do men and women differ in their drives and desires?

What Sex Is and Is Not For
10. What do the authors say that sex is and is not for? How do you feel about the list? Would you add others?

The Problems of Too Much and Too Little
11. Discuss the fictional wife's responses to her husband. Have you ever used, "Is that all you ever think about!" and some of the others? Why?
12. What can husbands learn from the discussion of the differential response of women? Do you think men are often insensitive? How can wives share this tactfully, so the husband understands and does not feel rejected?
13. Do you think that a couple's sexual compatibility is a good measure of their total marriage adjustment? In what ways does a poor sexual adjustment affect the rest of the marriage?

Intimacy as a Ministry
14. The authors suggest that husbands and wives do things for one another because they love each other. Often, they do things that they may not necessarily prefer doing. Do you agree that being sexually intimate is something a spouse should do for another, even when he or she may not desire intimacy as much as his or her spouse does?

Morality in the Bedroom
15. What is your reaction to the statement: "Anything that a married couple decide to do to pleasure one another is acceptable and right." Discuss any limitations you might place or not place on it.

Chapter 8. *Child Rearing in Marriage: Principles and Practices*
Put Your Spouse First
1. What evidence have you gleaned that confirms the authors' belief that children gain security from loyalty, affection, and love shared by one parent for another?

2. How does Mark 10:7 relate to the priority of loyalty, love, and commitment? Does this saying which Jesus quotes from Genesis 2:24 and which Paul quotes in Ephesians 5:31 support the authors' admonition to put your spouse first? In what ways should your spouse come first? In terms of loyalty, priority, time, and the like?

Parenting Models
  3. What types of parenting models do you espouse and practice: Martyr, Pal, Police Officer, Teacher and Counselor, Athletic Coach?
  4. How have your children been influenced by the use of the model(s) you have used? Are you happy with their development?
  5. Are there parts of other models that you would like to include in your approach to child rearing? What are they and how would you go about using them?

Principles of Nurture
  6. How do you handle discipline (rewards and punishments) in your family? What techniques and strategies have worked best for you?
  7. Discuss discipline in the light of Proverbs 6:23; 13:24; 19:18; 22:6; 23:13; 29:17, and Ephesians 6:4.
  8. Why is *unconditional love* vital for your child's wholesome development? What place do *trust* and *respect* play in raising children?
  9. Discuss *unconditional love* in the light of the story of the *Two Sons* or *The Prodigal Son and His Elder Brother* in Luke 15:11-32.
 10. How is "letting go" a vital part of unconditional love?
 11. The authors believe that even in the best of families children go astray and rebel against family values. Parents ought not to assume that it's always their fault. Discuss the various ways you believe parents should and should not react when children and youth rebel.
 12. Parents cannot give an equal amount of time to each child, since each child is different in personality and need. Nonetheless, partiality is something we should avoid. How do we go about loving each child according to his or her need?
 13. What can we learn from the experience of Jacob with his sons in Genesis 37:1ff.? Can you think of other cases, either biblical ones or some from your acquaintances, where partiality has caused conflict among children?
 14. Do you believe that you are giving enough time, both quality and quantity, to your children? What activities do you as parents do with them?
 15. How can we be sure that we are not rationalizing the matter of quality time?
 16. What are your family guidelines and rules? How will they, or have they, changed over time? How have your children been affected by these guidelines and rules?
 17. Folk wisdom says that we should make as few rules as possible, but that we should enforce the ones we do make. Do you agree or disagree? Why?
 18. How do you foster a sense of self-esteem and self-worth in your children? Share with the group how you go about doing this.

19. Discuss the need of children and youth for responsibility. Why is it essential to proper maturation and growth? How do we go about deciding how much to give them?
20. Should we check up on our children when we give them a task? Why? Why not?
21. What values are essential for Christian growth? What values have or haven't you taught your children through parental example?
22. Since other groups and individuals influence your children's values, how can parents influence children in their choice of their friends?
23. What part does family worship and "Christian talk" at home play in shaping our children's beliefs and values? How important is involvement in Sunday school and youth group?

Parents Have Parents
24. In what ways are you as adults and/or parents loving your own parents? Could you improve in this area? How?

Keep Laughter in the Home
25. Virginia Satir, in her book *People Making*, poses these questions about the home environment: "Does it feel good to you to live in your family right now? Do you feel you are living with friends, people you like and trust, and who like and trust you? Is it fun and exciting to be a member of your family?"

   How do you respond to these questions? How do you think your children would respond to them? Are these accurate measures of a good Christian home? Discuss. What do you do as parents to keep your home a pleasant, joyful place?

Chapter 9. *Infidelity in Marriage: Push and Pull Factors*
Kin Relationships
1. Why do the authors insist that our primary relationship should be with God?
2. Examine Mark 12:29-31, Luke 14:26-27, and Matthew 10:37-39. In what ways do our wife or husband and children benefit by our putting God first in our lives?

We Marry Because We Have Needs
3. We all marry because we have needs that we want to have met. What needs do you think most married people had in mind when they were looking forward to marriage? Are there needs that we develop after we are married that are different? How have they changed as you have passed through the various stages in the married life cycle? Share these with the group, discussing their relative importance.
4. Distinguish and discuss how the needs of a husband and wife

differ—from your perspective. In what order would you rank them? It is possible for us to meet all of each other's needs? Which ones, if any, are best met by others outside of the family?
5. The authors state that "infidelity to God may lead to marital infidelity." Why do you think they believe this? Under what circumstance would one lead to the other?
6. Can marital infidelity also lead to unfaithfulness to God? Discuss.

Spouse Surrogates
7. All of us are vulnerable to infidelity. What unmet needs do you think make us most susceptible to infidelity?
8. Do you have any "spouse surrogates" in your life that you can share with the group? Why do you think you turned to these surrogates? Was it because you felt some of your needs were not being met in your marriage? Was the surrogate the only alternative? Discuss.
9. What safeguards or steps can we take to avoid infidelity?

Change Is Constant
10. What words in your wedding vows actually should have alerted you to the fact that changes (suffering, as well as joy) would be part of your marital experience?
11. Discuss Dr. Foreman's statement: "I could never understand why I got along with some women better than I did with my wife until I realized that I didn't try to change them." Do you feel the desire to change one's spouse is indeed at the root of a lot of marital discord?
12. Is conflict inevitable in a deep relationship? Why?

Loyalty and Commitment
13. Why do we need to feel that our spouse is going to be loyal to us? Why is one hundred percent commitment by both partners essential to a stable marriage?

Push and Pull Factors
14. What are the *push* and *pull* factors that the authors identify? Can you suggest others that contribute to infidelity? Discuss the ways that Christians can manage these and possibly overcome them.

Adultery Does Happen
15. How would you handle sexual infidelity by your spouse?
16. Dr. James Dobson suggests that when a spouse is unfaithful, the unfaithful spouse should be confronted and given a choice: either repent and stay with his or her spouse, or leave. While this is difficult to do, he says that love must be tough. Discuss Dobson's concept of "tough love" as it relates to handling marital infidelity.

17. Is divorce an appropriate option for a Christian? Under what circumstances? What scriptural texts guide you in your decision?
18. How does our Lord's teachings about forgiveness relate to forgiving an unfaithful spouse? See Matthew 6:14-15 and Luke 17:3-4. What are the prerequisites for forgiveness (Luke 17:)?

Support Groups and Support Couples
Some Protestant and Roman Catholic churches have established support groups for newly married people. The assumption is that people do not become aware of the difficulties and problems they will encounter in a new experience until they *actually* enter into it.
Discuss the relevance of such support groups and supporting couples. How could you go about establishing such a group of couples in your church? Do you see both the newly married and those who have been married a while welcoming such a program?

SUGGESTED READINGS

Chapter 1
Bird, Joseph and Lois, *Marriage Is For Grown Ups*, Image Books, 1971.
Curran, Dolores, *Traits of a Healthy Family*, Winston Press, 1983
Ford, Edward E., *Why Marriage?* Argus Communications, 1974.
Glasser, William, *Reality Therapy*, Harper & Row, 1964.
Mace, David and Vera, *How to Have a Happy Marriage*, Abingdon, 1977.
Peck, M. Scott, *The Road Less Traveled*, Touchstone Books, 1980.

Chapter 2
Augsburger, David, *Cherishable: Love and Marriage*, Herald Press, 1971.
De Jong, Peter and Donald R. Wilson, *Husband and Wife*, Zondervan, 1979.
MacDonald, Gordon, *Magnificent Marriage*, Tyndale, 1980.
Olthuis, James H., *I Pledge My Troth*, Harper & Row, 1975.
Pope John Paul II, *On the Family*, U.S. Catholic Conference, 1982
Powell, John S. J., *The Christian Vision*, Argus Communications, 1984.
Scanzoni, Letha and Nancy Hardesty, *All We're Meant to Be*, Word, 1974.

Chapter 3
Bender, Ross T., *Christian Families*, Herald Press, 1982.
Lederer, William and Don D. Jackson, *The Mirages of Marriage*, W. W. Norton, 1968.
Levinson, Daniel J., *The Seasons of a Man's Life*, Ballantine Books, 1979.
Sheehy, Gail, *Passages*, Bantam Books, 1976.

Chapter 4
Dobson, James, *Love Must Be Tough*, Word, 1983.
Dresher, John M., *Now Is the Time to Love*, Herald Press, 1970.
Ford, Edward E., and Steven L. Englund, *Permanent Love*, Winston Press, 1979

Fromm, Erich, *The Art of Loving*, Bantam Books, 1963.
Lewis, C. S., *The Four Loves*, Collins, 1963.
Powell, John S. J., *The Christian Vision*, Argus Communications, 1984.
―――――――, *The Secret of Staying in Love*, Argus Commmunications, 1974.
Smedes, Lewis B., *Love Within Limits: A Realistic View of 1 Corinthians 13*, Eerdmans, 1978.
Stoesz, Cheryl with Gilbert G. Brandt, *The Struggle of Love*, Kindred Press, 1983.
Swihart, Judson, *How Do I Say I Love You?*, InterVarsity Press, 1977.

Chapter 5
Augsburger, David W., *Caring Enough to Hear and Be Heard*, Herald Press, 1982
Bach, George and Peter Wyden, *The Intimate Enemy: How to Fight Fair in Love and Marriage*, Avon, 1970.
Balswick, Jack, *Why I Can't Say I Love You*, Word Books, 1978.
Dobson, James, *What Wives Wish Their Husbands Knew About Women*, Tyndale, 1975.
Egan, Gerard, *You and Me: The Skills of Communicating and Relating to Others*, Wadsworth, 1977.
Miller, Sherod, et al., *Straight Talk: How to Improve Your Relationships Through Better Communication*, Rawson Associates, 1980.
Powell, John S.J., *Why Am I Afraid to Tell You Who I Am?* Argus Communications, 1969.
Schmitt, Abraham and Dorothy, *Renewing Family Life*, Herald Press, 1985.
Wahbroos, Sven, *Family Communication*, (Revised Edition), A Plume Book, 1974.
Wright, H. Norman, *Communication: Key to Your Marriage*, Regal Books, 1971.

Chapter 6
Augsburger, David W., *Caring Enough to Confront*, Herald Press, 1980.
―――――――, *When Caring Is Not Enough*, Herald Press, 1983.
Fairfield, James G., *When You Don't Agree*, Herald Press, 1977.
Leaman, David R., *Making Decisions: A Guide for Couples*, Herald Press, 1979.
Mace, David, *Love and Anger in Marriage*, Zondervan, 1982.
Schmitt, Abraham and Dorothy, *Renewing Family Life*, Herald Press, 1985.

Chapter 7
Bird, Joseph and Lois, *Freedom of Sexual Love*, Doubleday, 1970.

Grace, Mike and Joyce, *A Joyful Meeting*, International Marriage Encounter, 1981.
McCary, Stephen P. and James L., *Human Sexuality*, (Third Brief Edition), Wadsworth, 1985.
Miles, Herbert J., *Sexual Happiness in Marriage*, Jove Publications, 1985.
Rubin, I., *Sexual Life After Sixty*, Basic Books, 1965.
Wheat, Ed and Gaye, *Intended for Pleasure*, (Revised Edition), Revell, 1981.

Chapter 8

Balson, Maurice, *Becoming Better Parents*, Radford House, 1981.
Campbell, Ross, *How to Really Love Your Child*, Signet Book, 1977.
Carke, Jean, *Self-Esteem: A Family Affair*, Winston Press, 1980.
Dobson, James, *Hide or Seek* (Revised Edition), Revell, 1981.
Drescher, John, et al., *When Your Child . . .*, Herald Press, 1986.
_____, *Seven Things Children Need*, Herald Press, 1976.
Lansky, Vicki, *Practical Parenting Tips for School-Age Years*, Bantam, 1985.
MacPherson, Michael C., *The Family Years: A Guide to Positive Parenting*, Winston Press, 1981.
Shenk, Sara Wenger, *And Then There Were Three*, Herald Press, 1985.
Winn, Marie, *Children Without Childhood*, Penguin, 1981.
Ziglar, Zig, *Raising Positive Kids in a Negative World*, Thomas Nelson, 1985.

Chapter 9

Augsburger, David W., *Caring Enough to Forgive/Caring Enough Not to Forgive*, Herald Press, 1981.
Becker, Dennis, *Family Night at Home: A Manual for Growing Families*, Kindred Press, 1981.
Dobson, James, *Love Must Be Tough*, Word, 1983.
Smedes, Lewis B., *Forgive and Forget: Healing the Hurts We Don't Desire*, Harper & Row, 1984.

BIBLIOGRAPHY

Back, George and Peter Wyden, *The Intimate Enemy: How to Fight Fair in Love and Marriage*. Avon, 1970.
Balson, Maurice, *Becoming Better Parents*, Verry, Lawrence, Inc. 1981.
Bird, Joseph and Lois, *Marriage is for Grownups*, Image Books, 1971.
Campbell, Ross, *How to Really Love Your Child*, Signet Books, 1977.
Curran, Dolores, *Traits of a Healthy Family*, Winston Press, 1983.
De Jong, Peter and Donald R. Wilson, *Husband and Wife*, Zondervan, 1971.
Dobson, James, *Dare to Discipline*, Bantam, 1982.
_____, *Hide or Seek: Self-Esteem for the Child* (Revised Edition), Revell, 1983.
_____, *Love Must Be Tough*, Word, 1983.
_____, *Straight Talk to Men and Their Wives*, Word, 1984.
_____, *What Wives Wish Their Husbands Knew About Women*, Tyndale, 1975.
Egan, Gerard, *You and Me: The Skills of Communicating and Relating to Others*, Wadsworth, 1977.
Ford, Edward E., and Steven L. Englund, *Choosing to Love*, Winston Press, 1983.
_____, *Permanent Love*, Winston Press, 1979.
_____, *Why Marriage*, Argus Communications, 1974.
Fromm, Erich, *The Art of Loving*, Bantam, 1963.
Glasser, William, *Reality Therapy*, Harper & Row, 1965.
Grace, Mike and Joyce, *A Joyful Meeting*, Winston Press, 1981.
Kelly, Robert K., *Courtship, Marriage, and the Family* (Third Edition), Harcourt Brace, 1979.
Kephart, William M., *The Family, Society, and the Individual*, (Fifth Edition), Houghton Mifflin, 1981.
Klemer, Richard H., *Marriage and Family Relationships*, Harper & Row, 1970.
Landis, Paul H., *Making the Most of Marriage* (Fifth Edition), Prentice Hall, 1975.
Lansky, Vicki, *Practical Parenting Tips for School-Age Years*, Bantam, 1985.

Lederer, William and Don D. Jackson, *The Mirages of Marriage*, W. W. Norton, 1968.
Levitan, Sar A. and Richard S. Belous, *What's Happening to the American Family*, John Hopkins, 1981.
Lewis, C. S., *The Four Loves*, Macmillan, 1971.
─────────, *Mere Christianity*, Macmillan, 1964.
Mace, David and Vera, *How to Have a Happy Marriage*, Abingdon, 1977.
─────────, *Love and Anger in Marriage*, Zondervan, 1982.
Miller, Sherod, et al., *Straight Talk*, Rawson, Wade, 1981.
Molton, Warren L., *Friends, Partners, and Lovers*, Judson Press, 1978.
Nye, F. Ivan and F. M. Berardo, *The Family: Its Structure and Interaction*, Macmillan, 1973.
Olthius, James H., *I Pledge You My Troth*, Harper & Row, 1975.
Peck, M. Scott, *The Road Less Traveled*, Touchstone Books, 1978.
Pope John Paul II, *On the Family*, U.S. Catholic Conference, 1982.
Powell, John S. J., *The Christian Vision*, Argus Communications, 1984.
─────────, *The Secret of Staying in Love*, Argus Communications, 1974.
Reiss, Ira L., *Family Systems in America* (Third Edition), Holt, Rinehart and Winston, 1980.
Rickona, Thomas, *Raising Good Children*, Bantam, 1983.
Satir, Virginia, *Peoplemaking*, Science Behavior Books, 1972.
Saxton, Lloyd, *the Individual, Marriage and the Family* (Fifth Edition), Wadsworth, 1983.
Scanzoni, John and Letha, *Men, Women and Change*, McGraw Hill, 1981.
Scanzoni, John, *Sexual Bargaining* (Second Edition), University of Chicago Press, 1982.
Scanzoni, Letha, and Nancy Hardesty, *All We're Meant to Be*, Word, 1974.
Sheehy, Gail, *Passages*, Bantam, 1976
Skolnick, Arlene S., *The Intimate Environment: Exploring Marriage and the Family* (Fourth Edition), Little Brown, 1987.
Smedes, Lewis B., *Forgive and Forget*, Harper & Row, 1982.
─────────, *Sex for Christians*, Eerdmans, 1976.
Wahbroos, Sven, *Family Communication* (Revised Edition), A Plume Book, 1974.
Winn, Marie, *Children Without Childhood*, Penguin, 1984.
Wright, H. Norman, *Communication: Key to Your Marriage*, Regal Books,, 1974.
Yancy, Philip, *After the Marriage*, Word, 1976.
Zerof, Herbert G., *Finding Intimacy*, Winston Press, 1978.
Ziglar, Zig, *Raising Positive Kids in a Negative World*, Oliver Nelson, 1985.

SCRIPTURE INDEX

GENESIS
1:27 38
39:1-18 139

EXODUS
20:12 134

LEVITICUS
19:18 84

DEUTERONOMY
6:4-5 84

2 SAMUEL
11—12 139

SONG OF SOLOMON
.... 104

PROVERBS
3:27 134
15:18 102
23:22 134

EZEKIEL
18:1-4 18

MICAH
6:8 67-68

MATTHEW
5:48 22
7:14 20
10:37 138
11:29 155
18:15 142
18:21-35 151
20:25-28 83
25:31-46 134

MARK
10:6 38
10:6-8 .... 38, 106
10:7-9 18
10:8 38
10:29-31 77
10:42-45 83
10:44-45 39
12:28-31 .. 20, 77, 84, 138

LUKE
9:23 155
12:15 135
22:24-27 83

JOHN
13:1-17 39
13:34 20
15:12 20
16:33 155

ROMANS
5:3-5 .... 132, 155
8:17-18 155
8:28 18
8:31 77
12:3 91
12:18 75

1 CORINTHIANS
4:7 37
7:2-5 106
8:1 138
8:1-13 101
13:4-8a 68, 89, 140

2 CORINTHIANS
1:5-7 155
5:17 40

GALATIANS
3:28 40
5:22 20
6:2-4 131

EPHESIANS
4:26 102
5:21 .... 40, 142
5:22-33 .... 40, 83

PHILIPPIANS
1:29 155
2:12-13 21
3:10 155
4:6-8 89

COLOSSIANS
3:18-19 83
3:21 121

1 THESSALONIANS
3:3-4 155

1 TIMOTHY
2:9-15 83
5:8 ..... 17, 134, 135, 140

2 TIMOTHY
1:7 132
3:12 155

PHILEMON
1:15 41

HEBREWS
2:10 155
11:1—12:11 155

JAMES
1:2-4 155
1:19 70
1:20 102

1 PETER
2:20-24 155
4:16-19 155

GENERAL INDEX

Adultery, 10, 149-153
Affirmations (eliminate the negative), 25-27
  accept responsibility for behavior, 26
  positive and possible, 27
  present, 26-27
  spouse, 25-26
Agnostic, 30
Alienation and sex problems, 106-108
Anger, 99, 102-103
  can be constructive, 102
  common behavior, 10, 96, 102
  cool it, 99, 102-103, 106
  pride and, 103
Assumptions and faith, 30
Atheist, 30
Augustine, 33
Authority structure
  altered by Women's Movement, 54-56, 58
  in marriage, 82-84
    equal partners, 82-84
    head/complement, 82-84
    owner/property, 82-83
    senior/junior, 82-84
  must agree on, 82

Barclay, William, 40, 155
Behavior
  Accept responsibility for, 18-19, 26
  changed behavior affects attitudes, 62-63
  learning new, 42
  love is, 67-68
  reveals beliefs, 31-32
Beliefs (affect marriage)
  being aware of false, 22-25
    change inevitable, 23-24
    conflict and stress common, 22-23
    people different "off stage," 22
    suffering part of all marriages, 24
  can't make another happy, 18
  crucial to marital happiness, 10

live responsibly, 19
motivate behavior, 31
reveal our religion, 30-32
values and, 30
Bird, Joseph and Lois, 25, 86, 155
Biswas, Renuka, 66
Blaming others, 26
Blos, Peter, 128
Browning, Elizabeth Barrett, 61

Campbell, Ross, 124, 156
Campolo, Anthony, 155
Change(d)
  behavior called for, 46-48, 62-63
  constant, 141-142, 144
  growth through, 18-20, 26-27
  habits and, 31-32
  self, not spouse, 26-27
Chesterton, G. K., 155
Children (Child rearing)
  crave discipline, 123, 128
  find security in parents' love-bond, 118-119
  parenting models and, 119-123
    parent as coach, 122-123
    parent as martyr, 119-120
    parent as pal, 120
    parent as police officer, 121
    parent as teacher/counselor, 121-122
  principles of nurture, 123-154
    be example, 132-133
    be impartial, 128-129
    build self-esteem, 129-130
    family council, 130
    give responsibility, 130-132
    guidelines/rules needed, 127-128
    laughter/joy in home, 134-135
    "let them go," 133
    listen, 124
    nonjudgmental, 127
    open communication, 130
    overindulgence, avoid, 131-132

181

respect, 124
time, 125-127
trust, 124-125
unconditional love, 123-124
Christ and forgiveness, 35-36
Christ's teaching on "oneness," 18, 38-41
Church
  ideal expectations and, 56-57
  infidelity and neglect of, 139
  naive withdrawal from, 32-33
Coles, Robert, 155
Commitment, 41-43
  one hundred percent needed, 39-40, 142-143
  key to working marriage, 47
  love and, 64
  mutual commitment essential, 82, 84
  unconditional, 64-65, 76
Communication, 81-95
  defined, 81
  God and, primary, 10, 84-85
  hindrances/obstacles to good, 87-91
    authoritative position, 88
    blaming, 89
    constant arguing, 91
    continual interruption, 91
    double messages, 90
    erecting barriers, 87-88
    incessant talking ("babbling brook"), 90-91
    lack of selectivity, 90
    labeling and analyzing, 89
    playing it safe, 87
    mind reading, 94-95
    not listening, 88-89
    poor self-image, 76-77
    pride, 85
  infidelity and, 10, 143-144
  key to adjustment, 81
  reasons for poor, 85-87
    fear, 85
    insecurity, 86-87
    poor home nurture, 86
  rules for good, 91-95
    acquired in family of origin, 49-52
    accept responsibility, 90
    atmosphere, 92
    empathy, 94
    feeling good, 95
    listening, 94
    location, 92
    reflecting, 94
    self-awareness, 92-93
    send clear messages, 93-94
    talk about, 95
    timing, 92

  sex and, 106-108
Conflict, 96-103
  barriers to resolution of, 98-99
    blaming and name calling, 98-99
    extreme anger, 99
    failure to acknowledge problem, 98
    fatigue, 99
    focusing on symptoms, 98
    not accepting responsibility, 99
  basic and nonbasic, 81-84
  common to all marriages, 10, 20, 22, 96, 137-138
  causes of (See root causes below)
  danger of quick resolution of, 102-103
  management of, 100-102
    defined, 101
    methods of, 101-102
  root causes (See causes of above), 96-97
    conflict over goals and roles, 97
    finiteness, 96-97
    poor self-image, 97
    pride, 97
  sexual relations and, 106-108
  steps to resolution of, 99-100
    identify possible solutions, 100
    identify problem, 99
    implement solutions, 100
    rank solutions, 100
    review, 100
    select solution, 100
Crosby, John, F. 48, 155

De Santo, John, 130
Dickens, Charles, 140, 156
Difficulties in marriage (See Suffering in Marriage)
Divorce(d), 42, 138, 147-148
  infidelity and, 10, 152-153
  remarriage, 42, 57
Dobson, James, 133, 155-156
Dominian, Jack, 112

Expectations in marriage, 10, 44-59
  awareness after marriage, 47
  gap can be narrowed, 47-48
  gap with reality, 46-47
  illusions, 48
  infidelity and unrealistic, 144-145
  needs be met, 138-139

Faith (See also Religion)
  active, 31-33
  love and, 9
  more than concept, 9
False expectations, 48-57
  sources of, 48-57

American society, 48-49
  church, 56-57
  family, 49-52, 145
  media, 52-54, 144-145
  peers, 52-54
  Women's Rights Movement, 54-56
False ideas (beliefs) about marriage
  behavior "off stage" is faultless, 22
  checkups, a corrective to, 24-25
  conflict-free/perfect marriages, 22
  growth without change, 22-23
  suffering is avoidable, 24-25
Family
  altar, 130
  models provided by others, 30
  sex information and, 109-110
  traits acquired in, 42, 49-52
Flight distance, 86
Ford, Edward E., 151, 156
Foreman, Kenneth, 142
Forgiveness
  Christ and, 35
  infidelity and, 150-152
Freedom
  importance of, 19, 49
  peer influence, 52
  love, will and, 65
  not limited by family, 50-52
  personal, overemphasized, 48, 49, 53

Gap between expectations and reality, 46-48
Gile, John, 27
God
  beliefs about, 33-34
  communication with, 10, 84-85
  driving force, 31
  infidelity to God and spouse, 137-139
  kin relation with, primary, 84-85, 137-139
  love and justice, 37
  nature of, 33-34
  Scripture as revelation of, 32
  vertical relation with, 30, 138
Gratitude, attitude of, 36-37

Hillery, George, Jr., 100-101, 156
Hopple, Lynwood, 72-73
Humans finite, 20, 34, 96-97
Humility, 142

"If only" statements, 26-27
Illusions, 48
Infidelity, 10-11, 137-154
  active faith a safeguard against, 137-138
  adultery and, 149-150
  divorce and, 152-153
  handling of, 150-153
    repentance, forgiveness and reconciliation, 150-152
    separation, 152
    divorce, 152-153
  humility and, 142
  irresponsible spouse and, 145-146
  loyalty and, 142
  marital needs and, 137-138
  poor communication and, 148
  pull factors and, 147-149
    desire to "find self," 148
    easy divorce, 147-148
    outside recognition and strokes, 148-149
    permissive society, 147-148
  push factors and, 143-146
    boredom, 146
    irresponsible spouse, 145-146
    poor communication, 143-144
    unrealistic expectations, 144-145
  one hundred percent commitment and, 142-143
  separation and, 152
  spouse surrogates and, 140-141
  to God, 137-139

Joose, Wayne, 155
Justice (and love), 37-38

Kilpatrick, William K., 155
Kin relationships
  God, primary, 137, 148
  spouse, 138
Kintzing, Lenore and Richard, 75

Lamanna, Mary A., 119, 122
Le Masters, E. E., 119, 122
Leveling, 93, 103
Leville, Timothy G., 93-94
Lewis, C. S., 155
Love, 60-80
  adapting and, 74-75
  agape, 17, 138, 150
  as work, 60
  application to all of life, 16
  Christian versus romantic, 16-18
  conflict and misunderstanding not a sign of absence, 75-76
  confronts spouse, 37, 71-73, 148
  defined, 64-69
  don't fall "into" or "out of," 62
  experienced in God and Christ, 19
  God models, 11, 60-61
  God, source of, 60

God's unconditional, 37, 77
growth in, a choice, 65-68
headship and, 40
in four relationships, 78-79
justice and, 37-38
not an emotion, 61
one kind, many expressions, 66-67, 74-75
patience and, 73-74
Paul's definition of, 68
reciprocal, 75
responsible behavior and growth of, 65-67
romantic, 61-64
sex and, 106
state of "being," 65
two-way relationship, 28
unconditional commitment and, 37, 41, 64-65
validated by behavior, 67
way of behaving, 10, 60-64, 74
what it is *not*, 61-64
wisdom and, 69-71
words not enough, 67-68
Loyalty, 190
Luther, Martin, 138

Marital stability
faith and, 137
stress and, 137
Marriage
danger of pride in, 21, 35-36
idealization in, 63
none perfect, 22-23
skills for, acquired in family of origin, 49-52
Marital checkups, 24-25
Media, 52-54, 144-145

Nature of God, 33-34
Nature of persons, 20, 34-35
Needs of spouse, 138-139

Oneness, 10, 18, 38-40, 119, 138
Christ's teachings, 38-40
Sexual intimacy and, 106

Parenting models (See Children)
Parents
not always liked, 123-124
provide support for, 134
Patriarchal family tradition, 10, 40-41
Peck, M. Scott, 15, 155
Peer influence, 52
Pop psychology, 18
Powell, John, 155
Prayer, 36, 59, 79, 85, 130, 139, 153

Pride
causes conflict, 21, 97
danger of, 35-36, 58
hinders leveling, 103
insidiousness of, 85
obstructs communication, 85
rebellion against God and, 21

Reidmann, Agnes, 119, 156
Religion, 30-43
attitude of gratitude, 36-37
behavior reveals it, 31
defined, 31-33, 37
oneness and, 38-41
primary influence in life, 31-32
Responsible living promotes growth, 19
Roles, marital
agreement on definition of, 82-84
Christ's teachings, 40
church emphasizes traditional, 40-41
conflict and, 97
influenced by Women's Movement, 54-56
reversal of, 74
Rommel, Anne and John, 135

Scanzoni, John, 82, 156
Servanthood
Christ's teachings on, 38-40
mutual, 10, 40, 83
Sex
abuse, 109-110
misinformation about, 104, 109-110
Sexual relations, 104-117
abstinence and alienation, 105-108
act of love, 105-106
as ministry, 113
barometer of happiness, 117
children present and, 115-116
communication and, 10, 106-107
differing desires and drives, 108-110, 112
frequency of, 108-112
illness, grief, pregnancy, and, 114-115
lack of, and infidelity, 106-107
need for, renewed daily, 105
no solution to poor communication, 107-108
oneness and, 106
oral sex, 116
problem of "too much" and "too little," 111-113
vital to marriage, 105
what they are *not* for, 110-111
women's perspective, 112-115
Shakespeare, William, 79-80
Smith-Hinds, William L., 30, 155

General Index

Spouse
    priority of, 118-119, 135-136, 138
    surrogates, 140-141
Stress, causes of, 20-23
Submission, mutual, 39-41
Suffering
    can be reduced, 15-16
    defined, 15
    part of human condition, 16
Suffering in Marriage, 9-10, 15-29
    reasons for, 20-24
        confusion about Christian teaching, 20
        failure to adjust to change, 23
        finitude, 12
        pride, 21
        sign of growth, 24
        unavoidable, 22
Swihart, Judson, 74, 155

Television, 52-54
    catechism, 53
Theist, 30
Time
    quality versus quantity, 125-127

Values
    American society, 48-49, 57-58
    differences cause conflict and stress, 49-51
    influenced by beliefs, 30
Voltaire, 33

Women's Rights Movement, 54-56
Wahbroos, Sven, 81, 156
Working mothers, 126-127

Ziglar, Zig, 156

THE AUTHORS

Charles P. De Santo received his B.S. from Temple University (1949), and his M.Div. from Louisville Presbyterian Theological Seminary. He was ordained to the ministry in the Presbyterian Church, U.S.A. While serving churches in North Carolina, he earned the Ph.D. in Biblical Studies from Duke University (1957). Subsequently he earned an M.A. degree in Sociology at Ball State University (1968).

After serving as a pastor of the Leavenworth Community Presbyterian Church in Leavenworth, Indiana, he embarked on his teaching career. He has taught at Maryville College (Tennessee), Wheaton College (Illinois), Sterling College (Kansas), Huntington College (Indiana), and since 1969 he has taught sociology at Lock Haven University (Pennsylvania). While he teaches a wide range of sociology courses, his area of special interest is Marriage and the Family.

Charles also does individual and family counseling, and conducts marriage enrichment workshops in churches. (During a 1988 leave of absence, he served as Director/Counselor at the Somebody Cares Center in Columbia City, Indiana.) He and his wife of nearly four decades, Norma Arlene Michener De Santo, have four children. All are married and actively involved in the church—Stephen to Nadine, Deborah to Dana, Susan to Jack, and Tim to Dawn. There are five grandchildren. The denominations represented are Mennonite, Baptist, Methodist, and Roman Catholic.

Terri Robinson Williams earned her Ph.D. in Family Ecology from Michigan State University. Her research efforts have been in the area of family stress in the middle years of the life cycle and in sex role socialization. A member of the National Council on Family Relations, she teaches in the Departments of Psychology and Sociology at Geneva College in Beaver Falls, Pennsylvania.

Terri is married to Donald R. Williams who is a pharmaceutical sales representative. Both are graduates of Anderson College in Anderson, Indiana. She served as a short-term missionary with her family in Peru and on service missions to Panama and Bermuda. Youth work within a church setting is of special interest to her.